Hot
Kitchen & Home
COLLECTIBLES

30s of the 40s 50s
& beyond

second edition

identification & values

COLLECTOR BOOKS
A Division of Schroeder Publishing Co., Inc.

C. Dianne Zweig

Cover design by Terri Hunter
Book design by Lisa Henderson
Cover photography by Charles R. Lynch

Collector Books
P.O. Box 3009
Paducah, Kentucky 42002–3009

www.collectorbooks.com

The current values in this book should be used only as a guide. They are not intended to set prices, which vary from one section of the country to another. Auction prices as well as dealer prices vary greatly and are affected by condition as well as demand. Neither the author nor the publisher assumes responsibility for any losses that might be incurred as a result of consulting this guide.

Proudly printed and bound in the
United States of America

Contents

Dedication

Working on this book has been a precious reminder of all the years I spent in Grandma Sophie's red, yellow, and white kitchen in Brooklyn, New York. I would prop myself up on her overstuffed vinyl and chrome chairs to watch her in the art of making chicken soup. Sitting at the matching yellow Formica table, I watched in awe as she put on her pinafore apron and reached for her favorite paring knife. With the finesse of a master chef, she cut carrots, parsnip, greens, and onions into small pieces and set them aside to be added shortly to the water simmering in her favorite porcelain soup pot. First she needed to spread out a clean towel on the red counter and take some more feathers off the chicken. This prized chicken was one that she had carefully picked out just an hour earlier at the neighborhood butcher; you know, the shop with the chickens hanging in the window. When it came time for seasoning, she used the adorable hugging bunnies yellow salt and pepper shakers shown below, which I thought were bears until I began researching them for this book. To me they will always be bears, and they will remain in the family forever, as they are indeed very special.

As an adult, after Grandma passed on in her late eighties, whenever I discovered something that reminded me of Grandma's kitchen I had to have it, and you know the rest. My collection grew and grew, and soon I needed a shop to display all my treasures. So now you know how my passion for red and yellow kitchen treasures started.

Perhaps it is apropos to dedicate my book on kitchen and home collectibles to you, Grandma Sophie. I know you are right over my right shoulder, helping me write this book. Thanks for teaching me well.

Dianne

About the Author

Dianne Zweig is the author of *Hot Kitchen & Home Collectibles of the 30s, 40s, 50s* and *Hot Cottage Collectibles for Vintage Style Homes*. She is also the editor of www.iantiqueonline.com, an actively growing internet-based resource community for people who buy, sell or collect antiques, collectibles, and art. You can find Dianne's fabulous retro and vintage kitchen, home, and cottage collectibles at The Collinsville Antiques Company of New Hartford, Connecticut, a 22,000-square foot antique emporium with an in-house retro café.

Dianne is a member of The American Society of Journalists and Authors. If you would like to contact Dianne, email her at Dianne@CDianneZweig.com or visit her website at www.cdiannezweig.com and her blog at cdiannezweig.blogspot.com

Introduction

Writing this book was a ball from the get-go. Imagine spending your days going from one antique shop to another, or from flea market to flea market, adding more collectibles to your already enormous collection. How much fun could one have and still call this "work"? I knew, however, that when the time came to photograph, research, and write about my collections, that I might find all this indoor quiet time tough to digest. But that didn't happen; the excitement never ended. I had a terrific time doing this book, and I really didn't mind eating all my meals over my computer keyboard. Working on this text was so much more than an opportunity to write about popular kitchen and home collectibles of the 1930s, 1940s, and 1950s; it was indeed a fabulous journey on the retro express back to cherished times!

Before I could realize what was happening, I found myself smack in the middle of Woolworth's during the colorful eras. I tried to get back on this imaginary train and return to my home in Connecticut, but the train kept taking me to my childhood Woolworth's in Fresh Meadows, New York, or to my grandma's red and yellow 1940s kitchen in Brooklyn, New York, for some blintzes (rolled filled crepes) and applesauce.

So, if I may, let me extend an invitation to you to take a fantasy stroll down East 93rd Street, past Grandma's house, to "the avenue," where we will once again open the doors of our favorite five and dime and walk up and down the aisles looking at the housewares, kitchen accessories, textiles, appliances, sundries, vanity items, and toys that we remember so dearly. Since I can't really take you through the doors of Woolworth's, which closed in 1996, nor ask you to join me for lunch at its famous lunch counter, I can offer you the next best thing, a tour through the pages of my book. So, pour a cup of tea, get comfy, and be prepared for a sentimental journey.

How This Book Is Organized

Following some helpful introductory chapters on the popularity of dime stores with thrifty American families and how kitchens have changed through the years, I present the main portion of this book, the kitchen and home collectibles from the 1930s through the 1950s.

These kitchenwares, accessories, and household products will be covered in 11 distinct sections organized to resemble major departments of your local five and dime or categories you would see in an old Sears or Montgomery Ward catalog.

When relevant, I have shared with the reader interesting facts and commentary on important historical, economic, and social issues that influenced the manufacture and sale of products and materials during these decades.

I have flagged those items that are extremely popular and have included additional resources for readers who want to go further in their research of particular subjects.

Values vary from one price guide to another and from one region to another. Prices listed for items are estimates only and are based on my experiences in Connecticut over the last 30 years.

Please accept my apology if I inadvertently underestimated or overestimated an item's value or made some other error that was, of course, unintended. I welcome hearing from readers who may want to share further information with me. Please refer to the section About the Author to find out how to contact me.

I have tried to present a fresh approach to everyday kitchen and home collectibles, offering a sampling of treasures that are easy to find and generally affordable and represent many different yet related categories. Although Depression glass, Fiesta, Jadeite, PY, Holt Howard, and others are indeed sought after by many, I have not focused on these collectibles because they are amply discussed elsewhere and, frankly, have become a bit more challenging to collect.

Additionally, you will see that I comfortably use the terms housewives and homemakers throughout this book. These are terms that have attracted quite a number of sneers from women over the years. In keeping with the jargon of the dime-store era, I freely use these terms in my book, fully aware that these descriptions of women's roles would not be politically correct in today's parlance.

"*Quick cleaning with safety...* that's what I want from my cleanser!"

Dime Stores: A Hit with Thrifty American Families

Little did I know when I set out to write this book that my home state of Connecticut would play such an important role in the history of housewares, appliances, and the development of so many inventions that modernized the American home. The tin industry, almost unknown in the United States, started in Connecticut in the 1740s. Connecticut is also home to the brass, clock, and hardware industries. Many of your favorite housewares marketed under the name Universal were developed by the Landers, Frary & Clark Company of New Britain, Connecticut. Landers gained a worldwide reputation with its famous Universal food chopper. Coffee lovers can thank Universal for inventing the coffee percolator in 1905 and bringing the world the first automatic coffeemaker in 1941. Landers, Frary & Clark is credited with introducing so many innovative household items to American families from the 1930s through the1950s. In fact, the city of New Britain, Connecticut, 20 minutes from my home, held more patents than any other city of comparable size.

Perhaps it was destined that I would take on this task of exploring more about the evolution and distribution of housewares. These goods and materials were originally homemade and first sold on pushcarts by peddlers. Later, household products would be sold in smaller specialty shops, followed by department stores and then sold in five and dimes such as Woolworth's, McCrory's, Kress, Kresge, and Grant, or through mail-order catalogs such as those used by Sears or Montgomery Ward.

Five and dime variety stores were a big hit with thrifty families during the colorful eras of the 1930s, 1940s, and 1950s, promising fixed prices and plenty of imported goods competitively priced. Did I ever imagine that one day I would rediscover many of these treasures and highlight them in a book about kitchen and home collectibles?

Dime stores were fun places to visit, and we all miss Woolworth's, which closed in 1996. Everyone thinks fondly of Woolworth's as the store in which you could sit at the luncheon counter and enjoy a BLT, fries, and a Coke served by a waitress in a pink starched uniform. After lunch you could go up and down your favorite aisles and perhaps return to the lunch counter later for a banana split.

Baby boomers will remember that Woolworth's had the best toys, dolls, wartime souvenirs, housewares, sewing notions, celluloid jewelry, cosmetics, knickknacks, and Christmas decorations. Imports from Japan were very popular, and in the late 1940s Frank Woolworth made a deal with the Miyajima Family (PY/Miyao), a major designer and producer of dinnerware and kitchen ceramics, to carry its popular novelties. Today PY's anthropomorphic tableware, such as those cute fruits and vegetables with smiley faces, have skyrocketed in price. Collectors of these charming ceramics pay dearly for these adored and hard-to-find collectibles that were once easily found at Woolworth's. Another dime-store favorite that is sought after by collectors is Homer Laughlin's Harlequin, a lighter version of Fiesta that was sold only at Woolworth's.

As you can see, so many of the home goods that Woolworth's carried are highly collectible and are hardly a few cents anymore. The majority of the collectibles you will see in this book started out on five and dime shelves or came from mail-order catalogs. For the homemakers of the colorful eras of the 1930s through the 1950s, discount shopping was a dream come true. You could stock up your pantry, dress up your closets, equip your kitchen and household, decorate your home, sew your clothes and curtains, and care for and entertain members of your family with a huge selection of products, materials, and goods from your neighborhood variety or dime store.

What You Need to Know about Collecting

I am still learning so much about the collectibles I buy, and I have been a hunter, buyer, and seller of vintage kitchenware for decades. After a while, however, you do develop a sixth sense about the field and you do begin to spot the reproductions, fakes, and poor choices a lot sooner. On the flip side, you also learn how to make good choices and how to shop wisely. I would like to share with you some ideas about what I have learned about collecting kitchen and home collectibles over the years.

Buy What You Like

I am indeed partial to the warmer colors of the forties than the pastels of the fifties, and I have not yet jumped onto the bandwagon of sixties collectibles, which seems to be gaining momentum. Buy what you like, not what you think is in. Even though I thoroughly enjoy reading lots of home magazines, watching HGTV, and poking around eBay auctions, I rely foremost on my own intuition and personal taste when making purchases for my shop or home.

Tastes are not only personal, they are regional as well. Even though mid-century design and 1950s palettes and styles are hotter than ever in metropolitan areas or on the West Coast, New Englanders are not yet ready for pink and turquoise kitchens and bark-cloth window treatments. It is certainly okay to collect and decorate your home to suit your whims, but investing in trendy collectibles for resale requires a bit more attention to your individual market and options for resale.

Is It the Real Deal?

Today retro is in, and there are a lot of manufacturing companies cranking out products that mimic the earlier looks that were popular in textiles, ceramics, glassware, and kitchen accessories. So one of the first things I will tell you is that if you see a funky kitchen towel or a fabulous set of colored aluminum tumblers that seem too good to be true, you are probably on the right track in pausing to wonder if these dynamite looking "collectibles" are the real thing!

One tip I can pass on is to take a close look at what you are buying in good light (something you cannot do when shopping online). Open up a tablecloth or dish towel and check for stains, pin holes, fraying, and fading.

Does the item you are looking at show signs of age? When examining fabrics to decide if what you have is the real deal, look for original labels, yellowing, fold spots, worn areas, and stains. Even textiles in fabulous condition will look and feel different from the newer reproductions.

Many kitchenwares and advertising items of the colorful eras (1930s – 1950s) were made of metals like tin and aluminum. Canisters, bread boxes, match holders, trays, and cooking ware, for example, are all being copied today to resemble the older kitchen

look. If you are hunting for genuine collectibles, you may want to see some signs of age such as scratches, dents, rust, wear, missing paint, and a sense that these items were once used. Sometimes you will come across collectibles that were packed away in a box and discovered in someone's attic or basement untouched since the day they were first bought. You may ask yourself, "Is this vintage or brand new?" In this case, look for embossed logos of the known manufacturers of the time, original paper labels, and carton packing to help you determine their era.

Also ask the seller to tell you something about where an item came from. For example, perhaps you are at a tag sale and you pick up a cute pair of salt and pepper shakers with no markings or labels, but the seller tells you that her mother, now in her seventies, was given these adorable shakers by her own mother, who had kept them in her kitchen for years.

You have just been able to learn something about the age of this item. Listening to peoples' stories about how they acquired what they are selling is of course not foolproof, but it can be an extremely useful and helpful way to establish a time frame to investigate further.

In addition to textiles and metals, you will certainly come across a lot of kitchenware made of glass, plastic, and ceramic materials. Sometimes you may believe you have found a vintage item only to discover that the treasure you found has, of all things, a barcode, zip code, or message that "this product is microwave or dishwasher safe." Oops, you have found an item that was probably made in the 1960s or later. Unless that is what you are after, pass on this for now.

What Is It Worth?

I will approach this topic by saying that most of my kitchen collecting friends buy what they love and will pay a little more for something that they must have. Because paying a little more is still in the affordable range for most kitchen collectibles, the majority of kitchen collectors do not seem to be as concerned with what a piece is worth in the same way as one who collects high-end perfume bottles or antique jewelry might be. One can relax a bit more when purchasing an eggbeater for $16.00 versus buying estate jewelry. But I do want to repeat a point I made earlier: if something seems too good to be true, it probably either isn't the real deal or there is something wrong with the item, such as a hard-to-find crack or chip, a defect, a missing part, a repair, a mismatched piece, or the assumed age item is incorrect. I ask you to proceed with caution at these times, and to study the piece further or consult a knowledgeable person or resource guide.

In this day and age of internet auctions, plenty of price guides, and lots of television shows about antiques and collectibles, sellers are becoming quite savvy. Sadly, I must say that the days of finding a real bargain or buying a gem from a clueless seller are almost a thing of the past.

Before I leave this section, I want to add that prices do vary from one part of the country to another part. Also it is easier to find some collectibles in one region over another and when that happens the prices tend to be more reasonable, so keep that in mind when hunting.

Should I Buy It?

When I talked about signs of aging, I mentioned the typical changes that one would expect to find in materials that are 50 to 80 years old. Now the next question is, should you buy kitchenware it if it has rust or dents, for example? The real issue is, what do you want to do with the item? Another question is, are you buying it for resale? If the bread box you are looking at is being purchased to sit on a shelf for show only, then the inside condition will not be as critical to you as it would be if you indeed wanted to use this box to store away the family bread. Whether you are buying this same bread box to resell or for personal use, you still would want the price to be lowered to reflect the rusting interior, however.

When buying glassware and ceramics, be sure to inspect these pieces very thoroughly, running your finger around the rims and being very careful when taking off any lids or covers to look for interior damage. When you indeed do find vintage pieces, examine these gems really closely, as older collectibles often have chips, rough spots, cracks, crazing, and missing paint or parts. Be aware that when purchasing items such as juice glasses or beverage glasses that these items usually came in sets of four, six, or eight glasses. Prices should reflect whether you are buying a complete or incomplete set and what the condition is in. Sugar bowls usually have matching creamers, and many other kitchen collectibles are found in sets such as spice shakers, salt and pepper shakers, canisters, etc. When buying single pieces to make a match with a piece or incomplete set at home, be sure you are indeed buying the same manufacturer and era of production. Figurines and vanity items made in the thirties, forties, and fifties often featured young gals toting parasols or umbrellas, or a

grouping of animals such as poodles connected with a delicate chain; be sure your purchases are intact.

Plasticware of the 1940s and 1950s can be very brittle and is often found with cracks, scratches, and chips, or decals that are partially peeled off the surface of the object. Look closely at these delightful items to make sure you know what you are getting. A cracked plastic kitchen canister may not be what you bargained for!

When it comes to ceramic, glassware, and plastics, I am much fussier about condition than I might be with other kitchen and home collectibles. Here my advice would be to look at what you are buying in good light, and if you make a purchase, be sure that these items are wrapped very well for the ride home.

What if you find a great advertising box, magazine, catalog, or brochure, but the price tag is tightly taped onto the cover and removing the tag will surely damage the piece? Should you buy it? Be careful here, because when you try to remove the tape, chances are that you will be taking off the writing and some of the original packaging or surface paper. If the price is right and you don't mind a few blemishes here and there, then go ahead with the purchase, but if the item is destined for resale, think twice about this purchase.

Can Collectors Be Divided into Types or Styles?

Among bona fide kitchen and home décor enthusiasts, there are definite differences in collecting styles. A buyer may not only be drawn to shapes, colors, or patterns of a certain time period, but also may favor kitchenware, figurines, planters, textiles, advertising, etc., associated with a loved one or a cherished time in his or her life.

There are "generalists" as well as what one might call specialists among collectors. Generalists have a broader interest in what they buy and are apt to come home with whatever they fall in love with at any given time. I would still consider these folks true collectors, because they are always out and about buying something. Specialists, on the other hand, zoom in on a particular collectible or genre and tend to be very selective. Both groups, however, can be very fussy about how their collections are arranged or displayed in their homes.

Buyers may prefer one manufacturer over another, such as Homer Laughlin, Harker, or Universal, or enjoy accumulating collectibles from a certain country, such as Japan, Holland, or America. Collectors may concentrate on certain eras, such as Art Deco, postwar, or mid-century, and be quite loyal to their eras of preference. There are all types of collectors, and they are as interesting and diverse as the collectibles they are searching for.

Here's a tip for collectors who are just beginning. For those of you who use online auctions and are interested in particular color schemes, try putting in keywords such as "red vintage kitchen" or "green vintage kitchen." You will be delighted to see sellers that have showcased kitchenwares in lots arranged in color themes. Buying a group of collectibles in this fashion is a great way to launch your own retro kitchen if you are just beginning. Or, using the same formula, if you want to try to replicate a particular era but you are not sure what the possibilities are for accessories, use a broad search category such as "1940s" or "1940s kitchen." Remember as with any form of buying to read up on possible purchases before you jump in. Most important, however, is — have fun hunting!

Collecting by Color

Artists know that colors and color combinations create different moods and invite different reactions. There is a whole literature on color theory and color psychology and much interest among manufacturers, especially in the textile world, to have a pulse on color matters. In fact, in 1915 a trade organization called the Textile Color Card Association of America (TCCA) was established to chart American taste in color. This group consisted of industry representatives who would choose colors for the following season. It also developed a standardized chart of colors that garment manufacturers and allied industries could refer to.

In the context of the dime-store era, covered in this book, it is interesting to know that in the 1940s, the war influenced the availability of materials and even what colors would prevail. The U.S. Government War Production Board closely monitored the textile industry, reserving certain fabrics, textiles, and metals for military uniforms or equipment. In the spring of 1948, the Textile Color Card Association issued its color chart, and from this time we begin to see a change from the drab colors of the war years to the beginning of more colorful palettes.

Other industries were also greatly influenced by the war efforts. We begin to see major changes in the household products available after the war, which had numerous improvements. Aluminum, plastics, and glass are examples of materials that advanced greatly as a result of wartime technologies.

When the war ended, the postwar years saw a calmer nation ready for a return to family living and home concerns. Magazine articles in popular women's magazines shifted from subjects about how women could be thrifty during the war to topics about home décor and entertaining. Manufacturers encouraged adding color to the home and ran advertisements encouraging women to buy products for their "gay modern homes." Housewares, which had been softer in tones in the 1930s, were now produced in strong reds and deep yellows.

Garments were influenced by Christian Dior's "new look" of 1947, with colors of pale grays and blues; blues also found their way into home décor and onto industry packaging. There was nothing pale, however, about home textiles. Everyday tablecloths, dish towels, curtains, and upholsteries were bold, colorful, and often patterned with florals, abstracts, or whimsical themes. Color was everywhere, from outside packaging and advertisements to the products themselves.

Creamer, white background, Deco design, "Made in Japan" stamp, $12.00 – 15.00.

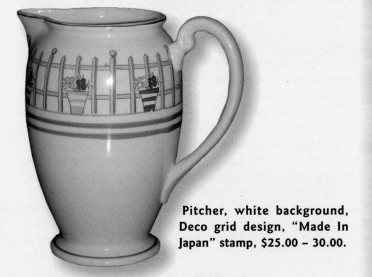

Pitcher, white background, Deco grid design, "Made In Japan" stamp, $25.00 – 30.00.

It's Cannon Color Magic Time!

Special values to brighten your home—lighten your budget!

1950s advertisement encouraging housewives to decorate their kitchens and bathrooms with color-coordinated towels.

When I set my Pilot's courses

U plan for **V** day

I WON'T ALWAYS be fixing things merely for myself. One day I'll be right on a major target—keeping house, planning courses for the grandest guy within Fortress range! I'm going to be an efficient housekeeper, and have leisure, too, thanks to Universal home appliances. I've already planned which ones I want to buy, and how to buy them —thanks to the "U" Plan for "V" Day. This plan helps you get started *now*. Here's how it works: . . . (1) Check on this page the Universal housewares you will need . . . (2) Add up their estimated values as shown here . . . (3) Put that sum into War Bonds . . . (4) Ask your local dealer today to put you on his priority list.

You make no down payment, you're under no obligation! But you do put yourself in line among the lucky "firsts" to get Universal products after Victory! *Send for the "U" Plan for "V" Day Booklet which gives added details*—write to Dept. UM

LANDERS, FRARY & CLARK · NEW BRITAIN, CONN.

CHECK UNIVERSAL APPLIANCES AND HOUSEWARES HERE!

UNIVERSAL APPLIANCES AND HOUSEWARES	1941 PRICE RANGE (Approximate)	ESTIMATED COST
Electric Ranges	$94.95—279.95	$........
Water Heaters	74.00—123.00	....
Washers	54.95—134.95	....
Ironers	34.95—104.95	....
Bag Type Vacuum Cleaners	29.95— 59.95	....
Tank Type Vacuum Cleaners	59.95— 69.95	....
Hand Vacuum Cleaners	14.45— 19.95	....
Landers "Open Top" Carpet Sweepers	3.95— 7.95	....
Irons	3.95— 9.95	....
Toasters	3.95— 14.95	....
Percolators	6.95— 14.95	....
Mixers	24.95— 27.95	....
Waffle Irons	6.95— 10.95	....
Sandwich Grills	7.95— 12.50	....
Heating Pads	3.95— 8.95	....
Hot Plates	3.95— 10.95	....
Portable Heaters	6.95— 10.95	....
Ovens	27.95— 44.95	....
Kitchen Cutlery	.10— 3.50	....
Carving Sets	2.95— 14.95	....
Table Knives and Forks	3.95— 19.95	....
Food and Meat Choppers	1.95— 3.25	....
Vacuum Bottles	1.15— 4.00	....
Picnic Sets	4.50— 9.95	....
Pitcher Sets	6.95— 15.95	....
Lunch Kits	1.95— 2.95	....
Household Scales	1.75— 4.95	....
Pressure Cookers		....
Fruit Juicers	3.25— 5.95	....
Stove Percolators	2.95— 6.95	....

TOTAL $........

BUY MORE WAR BONDS!

Check here the Universal appliances you've dreamed of owning. Put their estimated value into War Bonds—then after Victory, you can stop dreaming and start owning!

UNIVERSAL

Universal advertisement, 1940s, $8.00.

Kitchens across the Decades

Kitchens went through dramatic changes during the dime-store era of the 1930s, 1940s, and 1950s. To really comprehend all the advances that took place during these decades, it is helpful to take a look first at what kitchens and homes were like at the turn of the century. With this perspective in place, the reader will be able to appreciate why the 1930s, 1940s, and 1950s have been deemed the "colorful eras."

In the early twentieth century, before electricity and gas, housekeeping was very time consuming. The kitchen was a work area, small and dark, centered around the cast iron, wood burning, or coal range. The old-fashioned kitchen was separated from the dining room by a pass closet called a pantry, which served as a storage area for dinnerware, linens, and flatware. Maids and servants prevailed in the larger homes, and the pantry was called "the butler's pantry" and was an American version of what our English friends called the "serving room." This room-sized storage area often had a worktable at which the servants could polish the silver, attend to chores, and keep a distance from the fumes and grease of the nearby kitchen, as well as have some separation from the homeowner.

Storage was quite cumbersome in the older home. Often there was an area in the home, such as the basement, for cold storage, where perishables might be kept or an ice box or "cooler," a passage in the wall that allowed cool air to enter. Canned goods became popular after the federal Food and Drug Act of 1906, which brought safety and sanitary controls into practice. Packaged products such as cereal and other convenience foods were now available. These items were stored in a freestanding cupboard or closet in the kitchen. Hoosier cabinets, baking cupboards with porcelain or zinc pull-out work surfaces, held staples such as flour, sugar, rice, and condiments.

The room-sized pantry disappeared and was replaced by built-in closets in the evolving "modern kitchen," which could store all the new convenience products becoming popular. Many homes still had larger walk-in kitchen closets called pantries. Today, many of us are delighted to find newer homes with some of the features of the earlier kitchens, such as a butler's pantry, or even thrilled to find a closet with deep shelves to serve as our pantry.

The kitchens in the 1920s were almost as sterile looking as hospital rooms, with easy-to-care-for surfaces and an emphasis on keeping food preparation areas sanitary, as more was being learned about the relationship between improper food handling and preparation and the outbreak of disease. The early twentieth century saw the arrival of toasters, coffee percolators, mixers, waffle irons, and of course, the electric refrigerator during the 1920s. In 1927, General Electric's Monitor Top model with a compressor located on the top of the unit was a big hit.

Although gas cooking ranges were the housewife's choice between 1920 and 1939, even though electric models were slowly finding their way into the market, housewives were reluctant to switch over to electric cooking. Many preferred their gas ranges, which heated food quicker and didn't have the problems of the heating elements, which tended to burn out in the early models.

MODERN oil range
by PERFECTION

High-Power Perfection
No. R-879

HIGH-POWER PERFECTION *sets new world standard of beauty and convenience··*

● Acclaimed as the world's most beautiful stove! Pictures cannot catch all the sparkling beauty of its cream-white porcelain enamel finish. While increasing the convenience and bettering the performance for which Perfection oil stoves have always been known, this newest range now sets a new standard of beauty. The best quality materials and sturdy Perfection construction make this range an investment in satisfaction.

A hinged panel that opens snugly against the lower front of the range conceals five High-Power burners. These burners are as fast as gas, with the economy of kerosene. Each burner responds instantly to the slightest turn of its control wheel, offering a complete choice of steady,

dependable cooking heats at any speed from the gentlest simmer to a sizzling broil.

The roomy, porcelain-lined, "live-heat" oven is built at convenient height to save stooping. High-Power precise burner regulation makes it easy to maintain the correct heat for any oven task from custards to biscuits. Another feature you will like is the concealed, unbreakable, two-gallon fuel reservoir, easily removed for filling.

Visit your dealer and see this modern oil range, one of twenty-three new High-Power Perfection oil stoves.

———•———

Enjoy modern refrigeration. Chill foods economically, and make ice cubes with a SUPERFEX Oil Burning Refrigerator—a "twin" with the range in design.

Now you can have a complete Perfection kitchen. These two new beautiful modern products are perfect "twin" helpers for the rural home. Both were designed by the eminent industrial designer, Wilbur Henry Adams, in co-operation with Perfection Stove Company's Styling Department.

PERFECTION STOVE COMPANY
7691-A Platt Ave., Cleveland, Ohio

☐ Please send me the new High-Power PERFECTION booklet showing modern oil stoves.
☐ Also SUPERFEX Oil Burning Refrigerator booklet.

Name_____

St. or R. F. D. _____

Post Office _____ State _____

The mark of Quality

PERFECTION STOVE COMPANY

Perfection oil range advertisement, *McCall's*, 1936, $8.00.

1930s

"So inexpensive," says Mrs. Blake ... *"Easy to clean,"*

writes Mrs. Morton ... *"Such lovely patterns,"* declares Mrs. French

I just bought a Congoleum Rug for my living room—a big 9 by 12 foot size. I was so delighted with the pattern and even more with the low price. It was *so* inexpensive! How *do* you do it?

My Congoleum Rugs are so easy to clean, they're a *perfect joy*. I have three—in kitchen, dining-room and sun-porch—and it takes only about 10 minutes to clean them all!

I'm so glad you like my new Congoleum Rug, Marion. There were such lovely patterns, I could hardly make up my mind which one to buy!

What a happy selection Mrs. French made for her kitchen. The colors in her new Congoleum Gold Seal Rug harmonize smartly with her new gas range. It's the "Graylock," Congoleum Gold Seal Rug No. 402.

Every year hundreds of women write us nice things like this about Congoleum Gold Seal Rugs, in sincere little notes telling us of their personal experiences.

You, too, will find Congoleum Gold Seal Rugs a perfect joy. Their rich colors delight the eye. Their practical, quick-cleaning features make your housekeeping easier *every* day.

Right now the stores are showing many smart, *new* patterns embodying the latest decorative trends. Be sure to see them! But be sure, too, that you get *genuine* Congoleum —in Rugs or By-the-Yard. Make the famous Gold Seal your guide. No other brands can touch *real* Congoleum in beauty or service! Room-size rugs up to 9 by 12 feet, from $4.50 to $9.95—larger sizes equally low priced.

"Oxford," Congoleum Gold Seal Rug No. 692—for housewives who want something new in tile designs.

"Woodland," Congoleum Gold Seal Rug No. 694, went back to nature for its freshness and charm.

Old advertisement, $8.00.

1930s: The Streamlined Depression-Era "Modern Kitchen"

By the 1930s, the kitchen was being transformed from the old-fashioned kitchen to the streamlined modern kitchen, with time saving features, better organization, and much improved ventilation. The "all-electric kitchen" was promoted in popular magazines with numerous advertisements showing newly designed small and major appliances. Mixers were the homemaker's dream, now designed with numerous attachments that could sift flour, mix dough, grate cheese, squeeze lemons, whip potatoes, and shred, slice, and chop vegetables, and even sharpen knives. "Depression green" was the "in" color used on the wooden handles of kitchen utensils, on kitchen cabinets and tables, and on kitchenwares. Often accessories were cream and green, replacing the white and black look of the previous decades.

Other popular color combinations in the 1930s were gray and red or crimson, silver and green, pearl pink and blue, as well as the use of checkered patterns on textiles. Kitchenwares such as canisters and bread boxes tended to be softly painted, with perhaps simple decals.

In 1935, the National Modernization Bureau was established to promote modernization throughout the country. Manufacturers competed for better-designed appliances and kitchen accessories. Color began to enter the kitchens of the thirties, and articles in magazines featured decorating tips on color schemes and how to incorporate the kitchen into the rest of the home. The kitchen was no longer a workstation, but was gaining as much attention as the rest of the home. Small and large appliances were available in color, and Sears and Montgomery Ward featured colorful kitchen wares and japanned accessories such as canister sets, range sets, cake savers, bread boxes, and wastebaskets.

Appliances continued to be produced with streamline designs, rounded corners, and smaller proportions. The combination washer/diswasher was introduced, as well as the garbage disposal and the freezer for home use.

1930s advertisement, $6.00.

1940s

So we picked the one that

Stays Silent–Lasts Longer

(because it freezes with no moving parts)

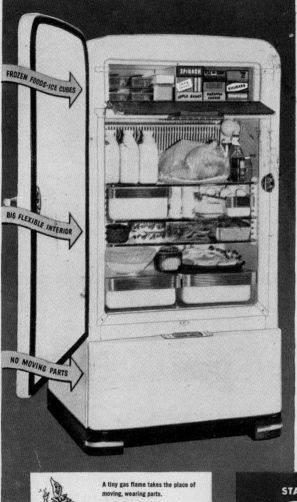

"**All the new refrigerators,**" say Mr. and Mrs. Francis Rheims of Brooklyn, "looked pretty much alike to us. All had modern features. But we found a big *difference* in the way they operated. We wanted a refrigerator that would never be noisy and would last us a long, long time. That's why we chose the Servel Gas Refrigerator." Servel has no machinery in the freezing system; no motor, valves, piston or pump to get noisy or wear. A tiny gas flame does all the work. So the Rheims family picked Servel . . .

. . . and got every new convenience

✔ **A big frozen food compartment**
✔ **Plenty of ice cubes in trigger-release trays**
✔ **Moist and dry cold for fresh foods**
✔ **Convenient meat storage tray**
✔ **Two dew-action vegetable fresheners**
✔ **Flexible interior with clear-across shelves**
✔ **Plenty of tall bottle space**
✔ **Handy egg container**

See the new Servels at your Gas Company or neighborhood dealer. And write today for new illustrated folder "Different from all others." It's yours free. Just send a postcard to Servel, Inc., Evansville, Ind., or in Canada, Servel, (Canada) Ltd., 548 King St., W., Toronto 1, Ont.

A tiny gas flame takes the place of moving, wearing parts.

STAYS SILENT . . . LASTS LONGER

Servel
The GAS Refrigerator

Servel advertisement, 1940s, $6.00 – 8.00.

1940s: The Postwar Colorful Era

The postwar kitchens of the 1940s began to become family gathering places, and now tables and chairs made of chrome bases with enamel, linoleum, or plastic tops could be used in these more spacious kitchens that had replaced the smaller work-centered earlier kitchens. Separate formal dining rooms were being replaced by kitchens that could accommodate families and guests.

The kitchen was becoming a very inviting space, and primary colors dominated the interior décor palette. Magazines advertised products for your "gay modern kitchen." Combinations of red and green and yellow or red and black were popular, as well as brightly colored tablecloths, textiles, and curtains. Flowers, fruits, and Dutch motifs were in vogue and were found on shelving paper, trim, decals, and kitchenware.

Old advertisement, 1940s, $6.00 – 8.00.

1950s: The Atomic Era—Pastel Colors & Space-Age Looks

Dramatic changes would occur in the kitchens of the 1950s as space-age atomic-era designs and materials entered the scene. The fifties kitchen featured plastics and pastel colors such as turquoise or aqua, pink, and yellow (cottage colors). Formica and chrome kitchen table and chair sets matched Formica kitchen counters and were easy to keep clean even if one had messy little ones. After the war there was more time for leisure, promoting kitchenware and accessories for picnics, barbecues, parties, and the home bar.

The introduction of color television in the 1950s brought full color into America's living rooms, where homemakers could now see all the exciting products and appliances available to them. Following World War II, there was a new generation of plastics and time for "gracious living" and entertaining. Kitchens and homes saw the transition from glass, ceramic, and tin products to numerous types of plastics that made casual living easier. Melmac and Melamine dishes, Lustro-ware and Tupperware storage accessories, and "Thermowall" for picnics were huge successes. Vinyl was used for tablecloths, chair covers, and furniture, and barkcloth with boomerang and abstract shapes was popular. Tablecloths and dishcloths continued to be brightly colored, and souvenir textiles were added to the home with tropical, Southwestern, and Mexicana themes. Poodles, roosters, and designs with kitchen utensils, teapots, and coffeepots decorated pot holders, appliance covers, and linens. Appliances were built in and came in fifties colors such as turquoise, soft yellow, pink, and copper.

As you can see, in a short span of time, kitchens went from the sanitized sterile white of the 1920s to additions of Depression green in the 1930s, bold reds and yellows in the 1940s, and finally, soft cottage colors in the 1950s. It should be quite clear by now that indeed the dime-store era was a very colorful period in the history of American home décor, often referred to as the time of "modern gay living." Retro collectors can truly have a ball finding home and kitchen accessories in so many different colors, patterns, and styles, as manufacturers were constantly introducing new and improved lines.

1960s: The Mod Kitchen & Home

The 1960s brought big changes in both the color and style of housewares and kitchen accessories. Combinations of bright ("Day Glow") orange, yellow, pink, green, and blue dominated the household palette. Besides wild and crazy colors, collectors will note that the sixties also was the time for major changes in textiles, furnishings, lighting, décor, and wall coverings. Patterns were often of optical illusions (Op Art), geometrics, abstracts, and, of course, vibrant flowers. Textile designers who worked for firms such as Heal or Conran captured the attention of the "in crowd" with their screen printed fabrics of contemporary designs. Psychedelic, swirling designs inspired by the mind-expanding experiences of the Hippie generation became part of the popular culture and were used on home and kitchen accessories as well as on luggage, clothing, textiles, posters, and even buses.

British clothing "mod" designer Mary Quant also brought her look into the kitchen, where her popular daisy motif could be found on toasters and canisters. Many people remember Mary Quant cosmetics, but her brand also was found in the kitchen. Colors of orange and sunny yellow combined with earthy tones dominated kitchen cookware and housewares. Accessories also included designs with whimsical mushrooms, butterflies, or vegetables. Le Creuset's cast-iron cookware in its signature orange color was found in kitchens abroad as well as in America during the "mod years." Ceramics, glassware, pottery, and textiles often featured abstracts and geometric designs and were made in bright colors or black and white. Heavy plastics was a popular material for 1960s housewares and furnishings.

Now that you have a bit more understanding about the changes that took place in homes and kitchens across the decades, you are certainly prepared to move on to the heart of this book, the collectibles with which so many of us are enamored.

1960s Mod-style kitchen.

Shelf Paper & Decals
Wax Paper
Paper Doilies, Decals, & Labels
Coffee & Tea
Canning
Pennsylvania Dutch

During WWII many materials, resources, and products were unavailable, as they were reserved for the war effort. For example, sugar, cork, and steel were in short supply, and these shortages impacted many manufacturing processes. Families learned to conserve foods and materials carefully and relied heavily on storage, recycling containers, preserving foods, and stretching meals.

Following the war, many changes took place that completely modernized the kitchen and meal preparation. Small and large appliances as well as numerous kitchen accessories and products were now affordable and available.

In the postwar period, the kitchen became a social gathering place where a person might share some conversation with a neighbor over a cup of tea and home-baked dessert. Women also enjoyed sharing recipes with friends. They compared notes on the latest cooking or baking products promoted in women's magazines. Pantries and storage tins were well stocked with everything the housewife needed to keep her growing family happy and well fed.

In the 1940s and 1950s, kitchens were colorful, playful, and whimsically designed with lots of themed accessories and matching products. After the war, families could relax and enjoy the comforts and safety of their homes once again.

Nescafé advertisement, 1950s, $6.00 – 8.00.

You **will** be able to serve home-canned fruits — **and the only limit is what you yourself put up this summer.**

If we knew of any way to spare you this hot, exacting work, we'd certainly never ask you to do it.

But this is war—and this is war work you must share, if your family is to have enough fruit next winter. You haven't much time to lose. Next month just about finishes the canning season. So — better turn to!

And when the war is won, Del Monte will take over again, *for good!*

Enlist now!

JOIN THIS DEL MONTE COOPERATIVE CONSERVATION PROGRAM

SAVE THE SURPLUS

IN

1943

You can't afford to overlook this, either

Now that you can buy so few canned fruits and vegetables, your canned food ration points are more important than money! You simply can't afford to risk spending them for a brand unless you're sure you'll like it. That's why it's sounder, smarter shopping than ever to get Del Monte.

OF COURSE YOU CAN STILL GET MANY

Del Monte

TAKE THE VARIETIES YOUR GROCER HAS

"FILL IN" WITH THE F

Old advertisement, 1940s, $6.00 – 8.00.

Royledge advertisement, "So..I'm a Spendthrift?", 1940s, $3.00 – 4.00.

Shelf Paper & Decals

During the dime-store era, homemakers had a lot of fun decorating their cupboards and storage shelves with brightly colored coated paper in common patterns of the times such as dots, flowers, fruits, Dutch motifs, Mexicana, roosters, stripes, plaids, and teapots. Often the shelf would be covered with this lining paper, which would be folded down to show a decorative border; or, separate scalloped trim could be applied to the shelf edge with thumbtacks. The Royal Lace Paper Works Company, in Brooklyn, New York, marketed this very popular product for the colorful kitchen under the name Royledge, advertising in magazines with the slogan "All My Friends Are Copying ME!" Nine feet of shelving paper sold for a nickel in the early 1940s and is very sought after by today's collectors, who can expect to spend $12.00 to $18.00 and sometimes more on these packages.

When women were not fussing with their kitchen closets, they often were busy preparing desserts and baked goods. Wax paper was a familiar staple often held in a wall-mounted metal holder, which also accommodated the aluminum foil and paper towel rolls. Please take note of the decorative wax paper shown later, which came in sheets, not rolls, and was a great way to jazz up dessert trays. When you finished serving your cookies or candies, you could store them away in a glass canister decorated with easy-to-apply decals that, like the shelving papers and trim, came in similar designs and patterns. Decals were also commonly used on bread boxes, napkin holders, and other kitchen accessories. In 1942, you could buy Meyercord decals for your kitchen or bathroom for 10¢ to 39¢. Now expect to pay $8.00 to $15.00 a package, depending on the designs. Decalomania of Chicago also featured decals, often with costumed people from different nations as well as other symbols of the times.

Royledge paper shelf edging, box with full contents, unused, bright sunflower yellow background with apples, popular in 1940s – 1950s kitchens, $12.00 – 18.00.

KVP shelf paper, box with full contents, unused, washable, turquoise/white polka dotted. 1950s-era shelving paper was a great way to dress up kitchen cabinets. $12.00 – 15.00.

Cut-Rite extra-strong wax paper, box with full contents, unused 125′ roll, Scott Paper Company, Chester, Pennsylvania, $12.00 – 15.00.

Wax Paper

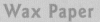

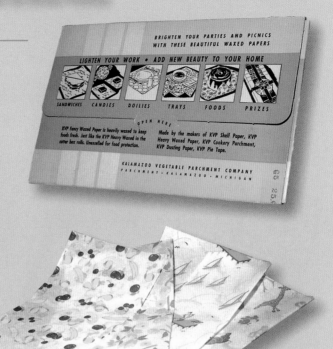

KVP Fancy Waxed Paper, box with full contents, 40 sheets, 11" x 13", originally sold for 25¢, boasting "5 Gay and Appetizing Designs from the World's Model Paper Mill" that could be used to "lighten your work," and "add new beauty to your home" and "sandwiches, candies, doilies, trays, food, prizes," featuring designs of fruit, circus animals, flowers, and abstracts. Kalamazoo Vegetable Parchment Company, Kalamazoo, Michigan, $15.00 – 18.00.

Paper Doilies, Decals, & Labels

All the packages of doilies, decals, and labels shown on pages 26 – 29 are valued at $6.00 – 10.00. Opened packages with single sheets bring $3.00 – 6.00. Reminder, when buying old stock of decals and labels, the glue may be dried out and you may need to be creative about using new adhesives.

Wear-ever advertisement, *Good Housekeeping*, 1951, $4.00 – 6.00.

For values, see page 26.

**Royledge advertisement,
Women's Day, 1948.**

Five & Dime Pantry

For values, see page 26.

Vintage image, *Better Homes & Gardens,* **1952.**

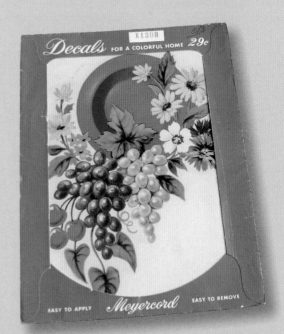

For values, see page 26.

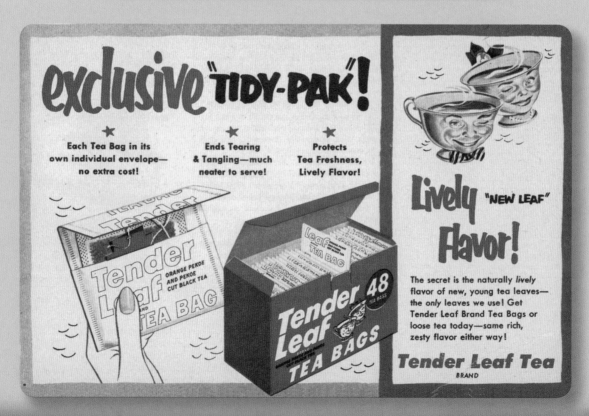

Coffee & Tea

Advertising tin, Swee-Touch-Nee Tea, The Consolidated Tea Co., New York, New York, $7.00 – 10.00.

Advertising tin, Savarin Orange Pekoe Tea, S.A. Schonbrunn & Co., New York, New York, half-pound, $18.00 – 24.00.

Coffeepot, glass with partial original Maxwell House red and yellow label, 1950s – 1960s, $12.00 – 15.00.

Advertising tin, Instant Postum Cereal Beverage, Post Food Products division of General Foods, made 50 cups, $15.00 – 18.00.

KEEP ON CANNING, EVEN IF SUGAR IS LIMITED!

Foods canned without sugar keep as well and are fully as rich in minerals and vitamins, the two things that make fruit indispensable to the balanced diet.

CANNING WITHOUT SUGAR

All fruits may be canned successfully when sugar is scarce by substituting hot fruit juice or plain boiling water for the sirups called for in BALL BLUE BOOK recipes, and may be sweetened when used. Select firm, ripe fruit. Prepare as for regular canning. Simmer fruit until hot through, in its own juice or in just enough water to prevent sticking. Pack hot fruit into clean hot jars and process in hot water bath (see BLUE BOOK) as follows: Berries 5 minutes; cherries, plums, peaches 10 minutes; apples 20 minutes; pineapple 30 minutes.

CANNING WITH HONEY

For acid fruits, make sirup of one part strained honey and one part water. For less acid fruits, such as peaches, sweet cherries and raspberries, make sirup of two parts water and one part strained honey. Boil water and honey together for two minutes. Simmer the prepared fruit in the sirup until heated through, then pack hot fruit into clean hot jars. Process in hot water bath as follows: Berries 7 minutes; cherries, peaches and plums 15 minutes; apples 25 minutes; pineapple 35 minutes. Only light, mild-flavored honey should be used. It tends to change the color and flavor of the fruit slightly, but the change is not objectionable.

CANNING WITH CORN SIRUP

Make canning sirup by boiling together for three minutes equal parts of light corn sirup and water. The proportion of sirup to water may be varied to meet individual preferences; corn sirup is less sweet than granulated sugar. Follow balance of directions for canning with honey.

JELLIES AND PRESERVES

Can the juice or the fruit without sugar; then make a small amount of jelly, jam or fruit butter as needed. Corn sirup may be substituted for as much as 1/3 the granulated sugar specified for jams and preserves; 1/4 the amount specified for jellies. Fruit butters may be made with less sugar than preserves. While sugar is limited, substitute these butters for jams, jellies and preserves.

For recipes and methods of canning fruits, vegetables and meats, consult the BALL BLUE BOOK.

Ball JARS, CAPS and RUBBERS

Ball jar advertisement, $8.00.

Canning

Canning is a method of using heat and airtight containers to preserve food. It strives to save the taste and texture, as if the food was freshly cooked. From the 1930s to the 1950s, home canning was simplified greatly by the introduction of electric food preservation using products such as the Ball Brothers Pressure Cooker and more efficient and easier-to-use glass storage jars, which had been around for awhile. Before modern methods for controlling heat for cooking were perfected, women stood over wood cook stoves or large kettles testing, stirring, and tasting, and then laboriously working to package their fruits, vegetables, meat, and poultry in all kinds of patented glass jars with specialized lids and sealing methods. In today's collectibles market, you will find a full array of canning accessories being collected, including jars, supplies, and recipe booklets.

The history of preserving our food goes way back to the Greeks and Romans, who used straw, rags, and leather sealed with clay, resins, and natural waxes to preserve foods. Over the years, cork, corncobs with cloth, parchment paper with egg whites, and wax have been used to seal glass jars. In 1855, Robert Arthur pat-- ented the glass groove-ring wax sealer. Glassmakers produced this product until 1912. Pre-Civil War jars were pontiled. The famous Mason jar came from the inventor John L. Mason. His famous "Mason's Patent Nov. 30th 1858" jar was produced up until 1920. In 1882, the Lightning jar was made with a new closure that prevented food from coming in contact with any metal. Similar to this jar is the Atlas E-Z Seal made by the Hazel-Atlas Co. Alexander Kerr's 1903 modification of the lid closure is closest in style to what we use today. In the late 1880s, the Ball Company brought mass production to the fruit jar industry (Milner, 2004).

There are thousands of types of canning jars and related accessories, spanning generations, in which collectors are interested. When approaching this area, be advised that there are many reproductions out there. When finding originals, value depends on condition, color, scarcity, crudity, closures, size, and of course, demand. When buying products in paper boxes, such as wax jar rubbers, make sure the boxes are intact and indeed older, as new ones are out there with bar codes! For more help on this subject, refer to some of the noted books on the subject such as *Red Book 9: The Collector's Guide to Old Fruit Jars* by Douglas M. Leybourne, Jr.

Ball jar advertisement, *Better Homes & Gardens*, $4.00 – 6.00.

Re-Ly-On "63" Home Canning Lids, box with contents, Crown Cork and Seal Co., Baltimore, Maryland, 1938, one dozen lids for use with 63mm caps and jars, $4.00 – 6.00.

Atlas Seal-All Arc-Lid, box with contents, used for canning and freezing, Hazel-Atlas Glass Co., Wheeling, West Virginia, one dozen lids with inside coating of impervious white enamel, $4.00 – 6.00.

34

Good Luck Jar Rubbers, box with contents, Good Housekeeping Seal, Boston Woven Hose & Rubber Co., Cambridge, Massachuetts, 1939, $4.00 – 6.00.

Ball canning jars with different lid types, $6.00 – 8.00.

Esso Household Wax, box with contents, for party candles, preserving, laundry, and household use, Esso Inc., New York, $4.00 – 6.00.

Gulfwax, box with contents, used for sealing glasses and jars, starches, and ironing. Gulf Oil Corp., Pittsburgh, Pennsylvania, $4.00 – 6.00.

Esso Household Wax, box with contents, for canning and other household uses, Esso Inc., New York, $4.00 – 6.00.

LADIES' HOME JOURNAL

Before You Start to Can
Send for this New
FREE CANNING BOOK!

Now! put up MORE and BETTER FRUITS with LESS SUGAR!

FINER CANNED & FROZEN FRUITS

You'll get Finer Flavor . . . Firmer Texture . . . Brighter Color

HERE it is! The new Karo Syrup Book that tells you how to can or freeze fruits so they're finer than ever before! All by using Karo Syrup and sugar, instead of sugar alone! And see how you *save* sugar. What's more, you can put up 20% to 30% more fruit with your sugar. In freezing fruits, you can save up to 50% of your sugar.

This big, 32 page book gives complete information on canned and frozen fruits . . . and on jams, jellies and relishes. It's packed with recipes—every one of them tested, re-tested and *proved* for you! For every recipe, correct proportions of Karo Syrup, water and sugar are worked out in simple, easy form.

This fascinating book is free! Send for it, now. Use it for fruits that look so beautiful you'll be proud to serve them . . . and that taste so delicious they'll thrill your family.

© Corn Products Sales Company

SEND THIS COUPON NOW!

Karo Syrup,
Madison Square Station, P. O. Box 342,
New York 10, N. Y.

Yes, I want the latest word on Canning and Freezing. Please send my Karo Syrup Book—"Finer Canned and Frozen Fruits"—at once.

Name_____
(Print Clearly)

Street_____

City_____ Zone____ State_____

Karo advertisement, *Ladies' Home Journal*, 1946, $8.00.

How To Can Meat, Game, and Poultry, recipe booklet featuring the "new" Ball steam pressure cooker, Ball Brothers Company, Muncie, Indiana, $10.00 – 12.00.

Recipe booklet, *The Family Food Supply*, fruits and vegetables in cooking, $10.00 – 12.00.

Recipe booklet, *Home Canning, Vegetables, Meats, & Fruits in the Flex-Seal Canner*, soiled cover, $6.00 – 8.00.

Recipe booklet, *Simplified Home Canning*, Hotpoint Co., full color, highlighted the Hotpoint electric range and how simple canning could be electrically, 1936, $8.00 – 10.00.

Duff's Hot Roll Mix advertisement, *Good Housekeeping*, May 1948, $4.00 – 8.00.

Sunshine Cracker Meal tin, red and yellow, $8.00 – 12.00.

Watkins Baking Powder tin, paper label, $15.00 – 18.00.

Davis Baking Powder tin, $8.00 – 10.00.

Spry tin, paper label, $12.00 – 15.00.

Egg carton, Deco style, $12.00 – 15.00.

Philadelphia Cream Cheese advertisement, *Good Housekeeping*, 1946.

Cottage cheese container, waxed paper, $6.00 – 8.00.

FFV Lemon Thins tin, $6.00 – 8.00.

Durkee's Mustard tin, $6.00.

Durkee's Pickle Spice, paper container, $4.00 – 6.00.

Sunsweet Prune Juice bottle, paper label, $10.00 – 12.00.

Assorted product labels lot, $12.00 – 15.00.
Courtesy of www.pinkgrapefruitstyle.etsy.com

Colman's Mustard tin, $6.00.

Stony Brook egg carton, $10.00 – 12.00.

41

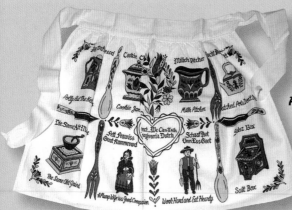

Apron, primary colors, white background, Pennsylvania Dutch symbols, $12.00 – 15.00.

Recipe booklet, *Recipes Made Famous by the Pennsylvania Dutch,* $4.00 – 6.00.

Candy tin, Pennsylvania Dutch Hand Made Butter Mints, $6.00 – 8.00.

Tin, Pennsylvania Dutch, $6.00 – 8.00.

Pennsylvania Dutch

The Pennsylvania Dutch are really not Dutch at all, but decendants of German farmers from the Rhine region of southern Germany who migrated to southeastern Pennsylvania. The official "Pennsylvania Dutch Welcome Center" explains the history of these immigrants by stating the following:

Like other immigrants, they brought their old world language, dress, traditions and art to their new home. Mystical bird and floral designs graced their birth and marriage certificates, family Bibles, quilts, and some furniture. The "fancy" farmers also decorated their large German style bank barns with colorful geometric patterns. Six-pointed star designs were very popular. The German word for six, "sechs," sounded like hex to their English-speaking neighbors. In time these "hex" patterns became commonly called hex signs. This custom persists today.

These bright, colorful designs had meanings or legends. Families selected a hex sign based on color, design and its meaning. Some of the more popular symbols included: hearts for love, birds (called distelfinks) for luck and happiness, tulips for faith, and stars for good luck. The colors used for painting were also carefully chosen because of their added meaning. Blue conveyed protection, white purity, green abundance, and red strong emotion. The hex symbols were individually hand painted

for many years. This approach, naturally very time consuming, limited hex sign use and enjoyment even in the Dutch Country. (www.padutch.com/hexsigns.shtml)

Pennsylvania Dutch kitchenwares, accessories, cookbooks, and décor are becoming of more and more interest to collectors. I have presented some very familiar items from the colorful eras. It wasn't until the 1940s that painters started to create hex signs that could be purchased and mounted on barns. Soon after, the symbols started to appear on packaging and advertising to distinguish products identified with the Pennsylvania Dutch.

Scholars have also suggested that hex signs were popular as a way to establish ethnic identity at a time when the Pennsylvania Dutch were being pressured to give up their German language and integrate into the public school system. Decorations such as hex signs and other décor were important to "Deutsch" immigrants because they promoted ethnic pride at a time when older traditions were being challenged.

When you think of Pennsylvania Dutch foods and recipes, you generally think of homemade and fine quality. Besides pot pies and lots of tins with cookies and candies brought from "Pennsylvania Dutch Country" by tourists, many cookbooks with favorite Pennsylvania Dutch recipes also made their way into many American postwar homes.

Cookie tin, oval with handles, red, Pennsylvania Dutch design, $12.00 – 15.00.

Tablecloth with green, red, and blue on white background, Pennsylvania Dutch design, $20.00 – 28.00.

Kitchenwares
Canisters & Cake Servers
Kitchen Storage & More
Canisters, Trays & Tins
Flour Sifters
Trays
Skeptical about Plastics
Pyrex & More
Aluminum
Retro Kitchen
Recipe Boxes
Planters
Mod Kitchen
Flower Power

Everyone remembers Woolworth's a little differently, but it seems that once you bring up the subject, you are engaged in a nostalgic conversation about the good ole days. What a treat it was to go up and down the aisles of the housewares department looking at all the colorful new kitchen and home products and décor.

In addition to neighborhood variety stores and smaller shops, peddlers, pushcarts, and open markets were all common places to buy housewares in the 1930s, 1940s, and 1950s. But what could be more convenient than the door-to-door salesman, who would come to your home promoting his company's wares? You could buy brushes, knives, home supplies, and cooking wares right in your own living room directly from company representatives.

Thrifty homemakers also took advantage of premiums and coupon offers for free products. Marketing all these "new and improved" housewares, soaps, and kitchen accessories was an important goal for competing companies that were interested in introducing so many first time inventions and revolutionary materials. To get the attention of prospective buyers, manufacturers sponsored radio and, later, television shows, flooded women's magazines with advertisements, gave out tons of recipe and instruction booklets, and offered numerous promotions and advertising items such as calendars, rulers, paper fans, desk blotters, trade cards, and more.

Kitchenwares

Tray, metal, silhouette couple, $8.00 – 10.00.

Scale, green, Chatillon, 1941, $24.00 – 26.00.

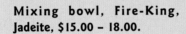

Mixing bowl, Fire-King, Jadeite, $15.00 – 18.00.

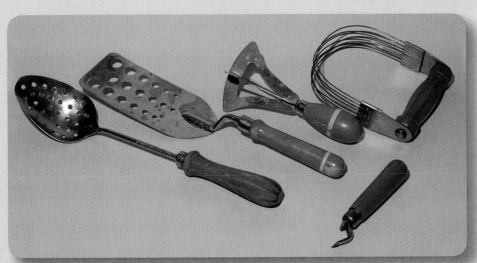

Utensils, green handled, rough condition, $3.00 – 6.00 each.

Canisters & Cake Servers

Kitchen canister sets and accessories made by the Ransburg company were of baked enamel and were available in many different styles and designs in the 1940s and 1950s. In this section I have showcased rooster-decorated products, those with the Chanticleer pattern, which came in matching accessories "for complete ensembles." A 1955 advertisement in *Better Homes & Gardens* magazine shows a canister, a bread box, a wastebasket, and a step-on can with the rooster hand painted on backgrounds in a variety of colors. Dark green or pink canisters are the accessories and colors I usually come across. Ransburg cake servers with the rooster design are not found as easily as the canisters and hardly ever discovered in yellow. To this date, I have never seen

the accompanying wastebasket or step-on can. I have also noticed that the rooster design itself may vary from canister to canister, and this would be expected in something that is hand painted. Please note that the deep coral and the pastel color are two distinctly different colors.

The Harper J. Ransburg Company of Indianapolis, Indiana, has a very clear embossed marking on the bottom of its products, in the shape of an artist's palette and which reads, "Ransburg Original Free-Hand Painted" or "Genuine Hand Painted."

These accessories were advertised to "bring the warmth and cheer that only color can give your kitchen," a consistent theme during the colorful eras. Ransburg was also noted for its bathroom accessories line, which generally had solid colors, gold trim, and no roosters!

Kitchen canisters, deep coral color, Chanticleer design, embossed "Ransburg Genuine Hand painted, Indianapolis, Made in USA," 1950s, $45.00 – 65.00 set.

Kitchen canisters, pink, Chanticleer design, embossed "Ransburg Genuine Hand painted, Indianapolis, Made in USA," 1950s, $45.00 – 65.00 set.

Dime-Store Housewares

Cake saver, yellow, Chanticleer design, embossed "Ransburg Genuine Hand painted, Indianapolis, Made in USA," 1950s, $35.00 – 45.00.

Kitchen canister, dark green, Chanticleer design, embossed "Ransburg Genuine Hand Painted, Indianapolis, Made in USA," 1950s, $45.00 – 65.00 set.

Bread box, dark green, Chanticleer design, embossed "Ransburg Genuine Hand Painted, Indianapolis, Made in USA," 1950s, $45.00 – 65.00.

Cake saver, dark green, Chanticleer design, embossed "Ransburg Genuine Hand Painted, Indianapolis, Made in USA," 1950s, $35.00 – 45.00.

"It's sweet of you to want to help but it's no work at all with Bon Ami!"

When a woman says, "Bon Ami is all the help I need"—she's really talking about something *much more important* than the ease and speed and thoroughness with which it cleans.

You see, Bon Ami is different from ordinary cleansers. It actually makes sinks and bathtubs easier *to keep clean!*

For Bon Ami contains no harsh ingredients. It doesn't cover the porcelain with tiny scratches that later catch and hold dirt. Instead, Bon Ami leaves a smooth, highly-polished surface.

From now on, protect your costly kitchen and bathroom equipment with safe, quick-acting Bon Ami.

Bon Ami
Keeps things bright
and so easy to clean

Why not "save" your hands?

"One of the nicest things about Bon Ami," women tell us, "is that it does not leave the hands reddened, roughened and scoured-looking, as gritty cleansers are likely to do."

Isn't it more sensible to use a cleanser that is easy on your hands—especially since it makes your housework easier, too?

"hasn't scratched yet!"

Copr. 1940, The Bon Ami Co.

Bon Ami advertisement, *Home Companion*, 1940, $8.00.

`Kitchen Storage & More

Canisters, white background, red flowers, red lids, Decoware, set of four, $25.00 – 30.00.

Canisters, white background, floral lattice motif, red lids, Decoware, incomplete set, $18.00 – 24.00.

Canisters, yellow, flower decals, 1930s – 1940s, probably part of set of four, as shown, $18.00 – 25.00.

Montgomery Ward catalog, 1950s, $6.00 – 8.00.

Canisters, Trays & Tins

A Passion for Fruits & Vegetables

Fruit designs and decorations were favorites in the 1930s, 1940s, and 1950s. Tablecloths, pottery, and kitchenwares were attractively decorated with cherries, apples, pears, pineapples, bananas, and grapes. Fruits represent sweet and pleasant times and are viewed as warm and home centered. Every culture has given meaning to particular fruits. The apple may be a symbol of temptation, but it is also a symbol of life, as it is a perfect fruit that carries its own seeds of renewal. The Hebrews view the pomegranate as a symbol of fertility. The Chinese accept the orange as a sign of good luck. Pineapples were symbols of hospitality in Colonial America. Fruit is celebrated as a luscious gift from Mother Nature and has always been a familiar image in kitchens.

Although fruit designs have been around for centuries, the dime-store years would be known for products and textiles that were hand painted, decaled, or printed with bold colorful fruit designs. Many attribute the abundance of fruit décor in the 1940s to the popularity of the flamboyant movie star Carmen Miranda, known for her fruit headdress and elaborate jewelry. She was the highest paid actress in 1944, dancing the samba in her vivid colorful costumes. In the 1940s, Macy's dedicated a window to this Portuguese-born Brazilian movie star who had a tremendous impact on clothing, jewelry, and style in America in that era.

Canisters, tin, fruit design, white background, red lids, set of four, $30.00 – 45.00.

Tray, Decoware, metal, apple and pear design, white background, $12.00 – 15.00.

Canister, Decoware, apple and pear design, white background, red lid, part of set of four. Single, $8.00; set, $22.00 – 24.00.

Canisters, tin, red with teapot decal, 1930s – 1940s, rough condition, probably part of set of four, as shown, $16.00 – 18.00.

Canisters, tin, white background, red lids, teapot decal, 1930s – 1940s, complete set of four, $25.00 – 30.00.

Canisters, hand painted, baked enamel, red background, flowers, embossed "Ransburg Genuine Hand Painted, Indianapolis, Made in USA," $30.00 – 45.00 set.

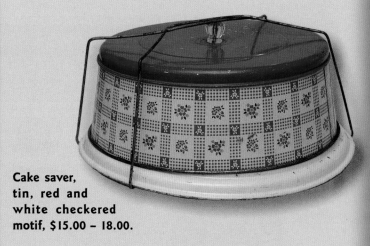

Cake saver, tin, red and white checkered motif, $15.00 – 18.00.

Here's all you do–

–dull aluminum shines like new–

DIP—The soap's in the S.O.S. pad. For economy wet only the edge. After use, leave pad sudsy and set it aside to dry.

RUB—Scour pan briskly at first, and then rub with less pressure, for S.O.S. polishes as it cleans. Quickly and easily.

RINSE—Rinse the pan thoroughly and it's ready for drying — prized aluminum shines again bright as new—lasts longer.

S.O.S
Magic Scouring Pads

S.O.S
Magic Scouring Pads
CLEANS AND SHINES ALUMINUM

*Copyright, 1941
The S.O.S. Co. Chicago, Ill.
S.O.S. Mfg. Co. of Canada, Ltd.
Toronto, Ontario*

S.O.S advertisement, 1941, $8.00.

Tin, part of canister set, red and white checkered motif, $6.00 – 8.00.

FLORENCE *automatic Gas range shown is one of a number of fine makes, made to "CP" standards. See them at your Gas company or Gas appliance dealer's.*

Look to GAS for the

smartest ranges of all

If you choose Gas, you can be sure of this: years from now, your new automatic Gas range will still be the last word. Inside and out, it offers you a clean sweep of surface that's both handsome and functional. You get such special Gas advantages as smokeless broiling, instant on-off heat, the evenest baking in the world. And you often get delightful extra surprises. The range shown above, for example, has a special new top burner with the "Governess" that controls the heat inside your cooking vessel automatically. Add the blessings of automatic cooking, automatic timing —and what more could you want in a range? Yet the new automatic Gas ranges cost less to buy, to use and install.   AMERICAN GAS ASSOCIATION

Only **Gas** gives

such matchless performance

GAS—the modern fuel for <u>automatic</u> *cooking . . refrigeration . . water-heating . . house-heating . . air-conditioning . . clothes-drying . . incineration.*

Gas advertisement, *Better Homes & Gardens*, 1955.

Cherry Themed Housewares

Flour sifter and match holder with stripes and cherries, 1940s, $25.00 – 30.00 each.

Canister, Decoware, cherries, $12.00 – 15.00. Courtesy of www.cottagerags.com

Soap box, metal, hand painted cherries, 1940s, $25.00 – 45.00. Courtesy of www.cottagerags.com

Dime-Store Housewares

Canister, $8.00. Courtesy of
www.onthecornervintage.com

Match safe, tin, $15.00 –
18.00. Courtesy of
www.vintagegoodies.etsy.com

Bread box, tin, floral, red and
white, $26.00 – 36.00. Courtesy of
www.vintagegoodies.etsy.com

Canisters, tin, yellow and copper, rooster
design, $18.00 – 22.00 pair. Courtesy of
www.vintagegoodies.etsy.com

Tray, metal, floral,
$8.00 – 12.00. Courtesy of
www.preservecotttage.com

Flour Sifters

Flour sifter, apple design, 1950s,
$15.00 – 22.00.

Flour sifter, Androck,
1950s, $25.00 – 30.00.
Courtesy of www.randoretro.etsy.com

Sifter, tin, white with
red trim,
$12.00 – 15.00.

Sifter, tin, red handle
and red, yellow,
and green flowers,
1940s, 6¼", embossed
"Bromwell's Super Sifter,"
$15.00 – 18.00.

Flour sifter, Androck, 1950s, $25.00
– 35.00. Courtesy of
www.cottagerags.com

Trays

Trays shown on pages 58 – 61 are courtesy of www.vintagegoodies.etsy.com, and are valued at $12.00 – 18.00 each, depending on condition.

O-oh, Mommy! That's COLD!

Sure it's cold—from top to bottom. That's "CIRCULATING COLD." Comes from the vented freezing shelves you'll find in Admiral's stunning new upright home freezers.

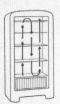

Without it you're getting only half a freezer. For only Admiral's "CIRCULATING COLD" surrounds and freezes every side of every package. Rock hard! Clear through! Sturdy pull-out sorting shelf for quick selection and arrangement of foods. Lots of other advanced features of convenience, beauty, economy, too. Well worth seeing at your Admiral dealer's right now.

Admiral
HOME FREEZERS

Three upright models • Three chest-type models

Admiral advertisement, *Better Homes & Gardens*, June 1954.

Advertisement, *Better Homes & Gardens*, July 1955.

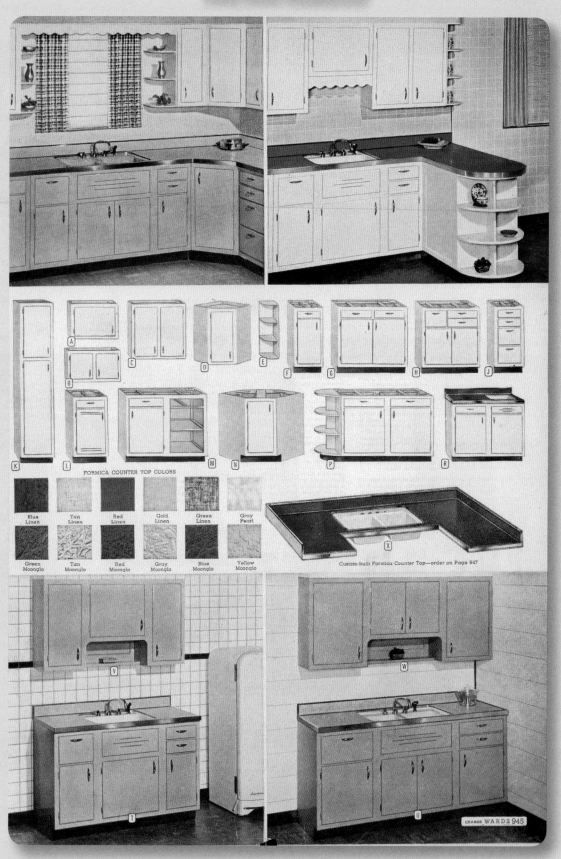

Montgomery Ward catalog, 1950s.

GE advertisement, 1950s, $4.00 – 8.00.

Styron advertisement, 1950s, $6.00.

Skeptical about Plastics

Believe it or not, housewives in the 1940s and early 1950s were skeptical about the introduction of so many plastics. In the 1940s, many smaller plastics companies were producing plastic goods that were poorly made, frustrating homemakers with these inferior products. Food containers would crack; toys, buttons, and dish drainers would melt; and accessories would fall apart. Kitchenwares wouldn't last over time, and the dissatisfaction with plastics was becoming an industry nightmare.

To counter this shaky beginning, marketing strategists decided to offer the public a new advertising approach, one that associated plastics with the attributes of old tradition and quality workmanship. Plastics were created to mimic natural materials such as bamboo, rattan, leather, tortoiseshell, or the finer kitchenwares such as china. Housewives were told that they could have plastic dinnerware that would be lighter in weight than china but would still have the lovely glaze of porcelain. To improve the quality of plastics, the Society for the Plastics Industry, along with industry suppliers, involved major manufacturers such as duPont, Monsanto, American Cyanamid, and others to help create and market better plastics.

Canisters, plastic, yellow, Lustroware, set of four, $25.00 – 30.00.

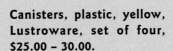

Bread box, plastic, red and white, Lustroware, $30.00 – 45.00.

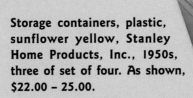

Storage containers, plastic, sunflower yellow, Stanley Home Products, Inc., 1950s, three of set of four. As shown, $22.00 – 25.00.

63

Canisters, plastic, pink, handled, coffee, flour, sugar, probably had one for tea. Set as shown, $25.00 – 30.00.

Flatware set, pastel plastic handles, Quikut, Freemont, Ohio, packaged, unopened, complete set, $50.00 – 75.00.

Sherbet dishes, plastic, Raffiaware, aqua and ivory, set of eight, $24.00 – 26.00.
Courtesy of www.modishvintage.etsy.com

Salt and pepper set, plastic, aqua, teapot holder, $22.00 – 15.00. Courtesy of www.vintagegoodies.etsy.com

Melmac advertisement, *Better Homes & Gardens,* **May 1958, $8.00.**

Regaining Consumer Confidence

The introduction of melamine dishes under the Melmac label was a big success. By 1952, the majority of department stores carried melamine lines. To boost sales even further, special presentation packages were developed that could help salespeople easily showcase products door to door or in smaller gift shops. These pop-up packages included easy-to-take-home plastic dinnerware sets that were far more visible and convenient than the larger, heavier cartons of ceramic dishes previously available. Colorful advertising along with easy-to-shop displays made melamine plastics an industry boom. (Wahlberg,1999)

Polystyrene Enters the Market

Later, other companies that had been around decades before used similar advertising campaigns, promoting better plastics with exciting promotions. Dow Chemical, maker of polystyrene powder, shortened the chemical name of its products to Styron and advertised its plastic housewares made of Styron in mail-order catalogs such as Butler Brothers. Styron canisters, pitchers, measuring cups, cake savers, and cutlery in bold colors were familiar five-and-dime and mail-order catalog products. Columbus Plastics Products Inc. of Columbus, Ohio, a company established in the late 1930s, saw its products climb in sales in the 1940s and saw an even larger boom

in business in the 1950s with the ever-so-popular Lustroware line, which had over 80 different kitchenware products available. In 1951, a Lustroware bread box sold for $4.95; today you can pay up to $45.00 or more for one in excellent shape.

The Catalin Corporation

The colorful eras saw many chemical and manufacturing companies revamp their earlier plastics in new ways. The Catalin Corporation made polystyrene, originally introduced in the late 1930s and reintroduced with "styrene" products, which were promoted as kitchenwares in "bright cheerful colors." Styrene, the shortened name for polystyrene, was used by many companies, such as DaPel Plastics, which produced its line of Chef Master kitchenwares, including condiment sets with its characteristic chef holding the plastic spice containers and its plastic chef spoon rest. Thermo-Temp made the Raffiaware line featuring salad and condiment sets and other popular picnic-related items. Thermowall construction provided better insulation and was made of plastic shells separated by air pockets. Burroughs Manufacturing Company offered its postwar Burrite Ware, which had smoother lines and was easier to care for. Early polystyrene housewares tended to be made with more angles, seams, ridges, and joints and were harder to clean. Postwar plastics were more durable and colorful, were smoother and easier to care for, and didn't chip, melt, or peel.

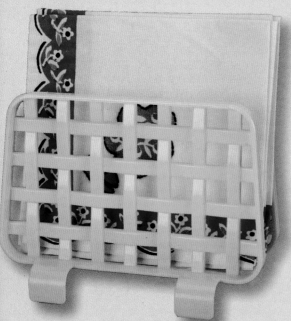

Napkin holder, plastic, yellow, $12.00 – 15.00.

Measuring spoon set, rooster, plastic, holder and spoons, $16.00 – 22.00. Courtesy of Marianne Dow, www. msdowantiques.com

Tupperware

Before leaving this discussion on the variety of plastic kitchen products that were available, I must include another famous plastic houseware — Tupperware. Chemist Earl S. Tupper introduced his polyethylene kitchenwares in 1945. These frosted, translucent, pastel products were known for their patented airtight seals and originally appeared in retail stores. Poor sales warranted a drastic change in how Tupperware was distributed, and in 1951 the "home party" was born, a throwback to the days of Club Aluminum's successful home sales.

Surrounded by Plastics — Especially Melamine

In the 1950s, homemakers were surrounded by vinyl wallpaper, plastic kitchen accessories, Formica countertops, quilted vinyl appliance covers, chrome and Formica tables with vinyl-covered chairs, and atomic-era plastic dinnerware. There were dozens of companies introducing their versions of plastic dinnerware, often referred to collectively as Melmac or melamine, even though Melmac is only one kind of melamine dinnerware product. Organic formed shapes of pastel materials were popular lines of the Booton Company, makers of plastic dinnerware. Booton also introduced the "square circle," designed by Belle Kogan. Brookpark, another noted company, produced square plates. Russel Wright produced shapes that captured its successful earthenware lines, and these items are harder to find than others mentioned. Other manufacturers that made melamine dishes were Aztec, Texas Ware, Imperial Ware, and dozens more. Auctions on eBay for melamine dishes can be quite active, especially for full sets or unusual shapes and styles. Be careful when buying these products to watch out for utensil marks, staining, dulling, and worn areas in the interiors and on the outer surfaces of the dishes. Take some time to acquaint yourself with the different manufacturers and to become familiar with which items are common versus those that hardly show up for sale.

Plate, cup, and saucer, Melmac, Windsor, $12.00 – 15.00. Courtesy of www.vintagegoodies.etsy.com

Cups, Melmac, assorted colors, set of four, $12.00. Courtesy of www.randomretro.etsy.com

Extra Smart! PYREX WARE in COLOR!

you'll use each dish a dozen ways!

IMAGINE THESE beautiful dishes on *your* table . . . they're strikingly designed, vibrant with color, real "show-off" pieces when you're entertaining.

And think of what a joy they are to own . . . for they're honest-to-goodness *Pyrex Ware!*

All of these sturdy beauties go in the oven, then right to the table! Any leftovers? Put your Pyrex Ware dish in the refrigerator, ready to heat up again.

Illustrated above: the new Pyrex *Color* Ware Casserole Set . . . a 1½-quart casserole complete with cover and four individual dishes (7-ounce size). In gay red or sunny yellow.

Pyrex Color Ware Casserole Set, complete **$2.95**

Additional individual dishes **29¢** each

2½-quart bowl with four 12-ounce dishes. Red or yellow.
Oven-and-Table Set,
$2.95

4 gay-colored dishes with clear glass covers. For baking, serving, storing.
Oven-and-Refrigerator Set,
$2.95

Wonderful mixing bowls to use a dozen ways. A size for every use.
Color Bowl Set,
$2.95

2½-quart size for buffet suppers. Bake in it, serve in it. Red or yellow.
Covered Casserole,
$2.25

PYREX WARE A PRODUCT OF CORNING GLASS WORKS

"Pyrex" is a registered trade-mark in the U. S. of Corning Glass Works, Corning, N. Y.

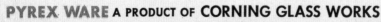

Pyrex Ware advertisement, *Good Housekeeping*, 1951, $6.00 – 8.00.

Pyrex & More

The Corning Glass Works Company introduced Pyrex oven-ware in 1915, licensing several glass companies to produce its product. In 1936, Pyrex Flameware was available, which expanded Pyrex from baking to stove top. Corning Ware, which could handle temperature changes like no other product before and was an invention derived from space-age technology, was introduced in 1958. Later Corning would market its Cook-Ahead Sets, allowing the same products to go directly from the freezer to the range and onto the table and which were first introduced in smaller versions as "oven and refrigerator sets."

In 1951, Corning Glass Works advertised "oven and refrigerator sets" for $2.95 that had "4 gay-colored" dishes, with clear covers, that could be used for baking, serving, and storing. I have shown the pastel versions of these refrigerator dishes, as they are commonly called. They were first introduced in yellow, red, green, and blue, with coordinating bowls and baking dishes. These Pyrex favorites were available in other colors and styles such as pastels and desert colors, and with designs. When buying Pyrex collectibles take the glass lids off very carefully and run your finger around the interior edges of the bases as well as the lids, checking for rough edges indicating chips in the glass. Often you will find that sellers put together their own "oven and refrigerator sets," combining dishes that are not really mates. Once again, advertisements of Pyrex products, like other housewares, can be found in old magazines, especially *Family Circle*, and are a helpful way to research products.

Mixing bowls, Pyrex, set of four, primary colors, $35.00 – 45.00. Courtesy of The Old Carriage Shop Antiques Center, Bantam, Connecticut.

Bowls, Pyrex, red and blue, 2½-quart; yellow, 1½-quart. $12.00 – 20.00 each. Courtesy of www.randomretro.etsy.com

Morris Metric Vegetable Slicer, box with contents, the American Inventors Institute, Asbury, New Jersey, $6.00 – 8.00.

Percomatic Baster, the Paul V. Shell Co., Kansas, Missouri, 1948, $4.00 – 6.00.

Villa French Fried Potato Cutter, box with contents, featured stainless steel blades, made in England, $8.00 – 12.00.

Grater and Pan Set, box with contents, aluminum, $8.00 – 10.00.

1940s kitchen, illustration, $6.00 – 8.00.

Cake Decorator, aluminum, $6.00 – 8.00.

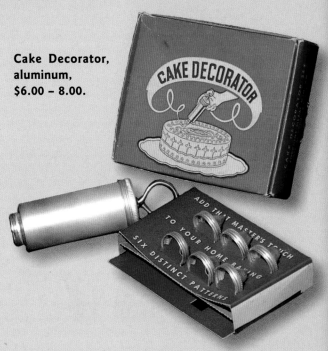

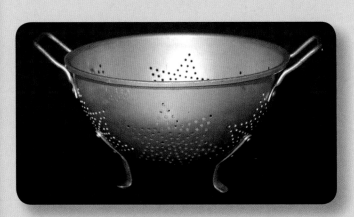

Colander, metal, unmarked, $6.00 – 8.00.

West Bend advertisement, *Better Homes & Gardens*, December 1952, $6.00 – 8.00.

Aluminum

Tumblers, anodized aluminum, "Sunburst,"
1950s, set of six, $25.00 – 35.00. Courtesy
of www.ImSoVintage.etsy.com

Coffee percolator, West Bend,
anodized aluminum, red, complete with cord and inserts, $18.00
– 26.00. Incomplete as shown,
$10.00 – 20.00.
Courtesy of www.fishlegs.etsy.com

Spice set and rack, Kromex, aluminum, eight
brushed aluminum round containers, labeled
mustard, allspice, cayenne, paprika, cloves,
nutmeg, ginger, and cinnamon, $40.00 –
65.00. Courtesy of www.elvisgrl63.etsy.com

Canisters, anodized aluminum, copper
color, $15.00 pair.
Courtesy of www.raraeaves.etsy.com

Retro Kitchen

Retro coffee carafe, tempered glass and plastic with candleholder stand, marked "Inland Glass. C.," $45.00 – 55.00. Courtesy of Sharon Potts, www.kitschykoo.com

Beverage glasses, Boomerang pattern, $8.00 each. Courtesy of www.TheWhiteMole.etsy.com

Serving dish, 12" x 12", tempered glass, signed Fred Press, $20.00 – 25.00. Courtesy of Sharon Potts, www.kitschykoo.com

Close-up of signature.

Advertising brochure, Vernon's Heavenly Days dinnerware, $3.00.

Advertising brochure, California Aztec dinnerware by Metlox, $3.00.

Sifter, metal, white background with turquoise pattern, Androck, $12.00 – 15.00.

Dishes, ceramic, white with turquoise design, assorted, $4.00 – 6.00 each.

Gadgets

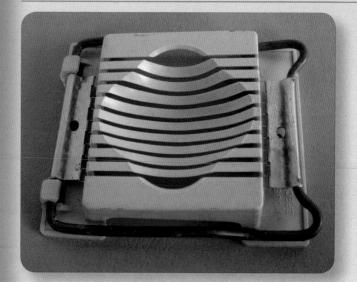

Egg slicer, aqua, plastic, $8.00. Courtesy of www.vintagegoodies.etsy.com

Can opener, packaged, $10.00 – 12.00.

Kitchen timer, tomato, $10.00 – 12.00. Courtesy of www.vintagegoodies.etsy.com

Lattice Pie-Top Cutter, plastic, $10.00 – 12.00. Courtesy of www.vintagegoodies.etsy.com

Recipe Boxes

Did you know that many of the older toy companies are also known for making recipe boxes? Recipe boxes are popular items on eBay auctions, especially if they are older and uniquely lithographed boxes made by J. Chein & Company or the Ohio Art Company. These came in numerous patterns. Many companies besides Chein and Ohio Art produced tin recipe boxes with whimsical designs. Stylecraft's rooster motif is shown on this page. Other popular designs by companies were kitchen utensils, plaids, and teapots. Recipe boxes were also made to be part of matching accessories accompanying canister and bread box ensembles or range sets. Ransburg's hand-painted enameled recipe box with a floral design in a variety of backgrounds is also sought after. Several of these are shown throughout the book. Over the years, tin recipe boxes could be found as promotional items from noted companies such as Heinz, Campbell's, General Mills, and others. These tins were mostly produced later than the 1950s. Recipe holders or boxes from the 1930s are made of heavier tin or wood and are plainer, with perhaps outside writing which might say something like "Recipes Tried and True." The 1940s and 1950s had a mix of wooden and tin boxes, but these were eventually followed by more and more plastics throughout the 1950s and beyond.

Recipe box, tin, rooster on white background, Stylecraft of Baltimore, $10.00 – 15.00.

Match holder, Ransburg, hand-painted floral, black background, 1940s – 1950s, shown with a matching recipe box and has other matching accessories not shown. Either piece sold separately, $25.00.

Recipe holder, baked enamelware, yellow background with flowers, Ransburg, $20.00 – 22.00.

Planters

Planters, glass, pastel colors, $8.00 – 10.00 each.

Anchorglass *takes the splatter out of mixing!*

At last! AMAZING DEEP-BOWL SET
DESIGNED FOR *Splash-proof* MIXING!

TULIP SET...1, 2, 3, 4 QT. BOWLS SMARTLY PACKED IN GIFT CARTON

4-PIECE SETS ABOUT $2.95

DEEP sides and tapered shape of these bowls prevent splashing! No more wiping splatters from walls, counter, floor!

You'll find these brand-new Anchor-glass splash-proof bowls rest on a good, firm base; perfectly balanced for tip-proof beating. Whether you use a wooden spoon, wire whisk, hand beater or portable electric mixer, you can reach every bit of batter without fear of splashing.

Notice the tapered sides. They make these bowls easy to hold, pour from, clean. You can even bake in amazing Anchorglass! So handsome, you'll use them as serving bowls, too!

See these remarkable mixing bowls wherever glass is sold. If your dealer does not have them in stock, he can get them for you by writing Anchor Hocking Glass Corporation.

● BLACK POLKA DOTS
1, 2, 3, 4 QT. BOWLS

● RED POLKA DOTS
1, 2, 3, 4 QT. BOWLS

Smartly packed in gift carton, about $2.95

Look for the name **Anchorglass**

MAY 1954

A PRODUCT OF ANCHOR HOCKING GLASS CORPORATION, LANCASTER, OHIO

19

Anchorglass advertisement, *Family Circle*, 1954, $6.00 – 8.00.

Bowl, Universal, orange tulips, $25.00 – 30.00.

Bowl, Fire-King Tulip Set #3. Single, $15.00 – 18.00; set of four, $45.00 – 65.00.

Flatware tray, wooden, $15.00 – 18.00.

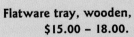

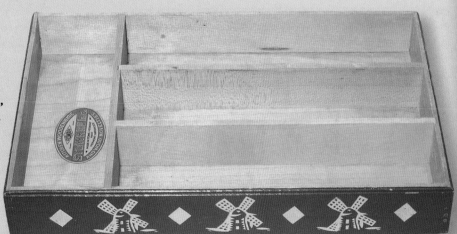

Dime-Store Housewares

Glasses, striped, $6.00 – 8.00 each.

Beverage pitcher, striped, $18.00 – 24.00. Courtesy of www.antiquesonfarmington.com

Syrup pitcher, glass, plastic green top, $10.00 – 12.00.

Jar, frosted glass, floral, Hazel-Atlas, $18.00 – 24.00. Courtesy of www.thebuttercup.etsy.com

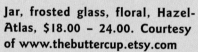

Beverage glasses, yellow striped, $6.00 – 8.00 each.

Coffee cup, red and white striped, Hazel-Atlas candy stripe pattern, $7.00 – 8.00. Courtesy of www.thebuttercup.etsy.com

Rooster, ceramic, $15.00 – 18.00.

Mixing bowl, 2 qt., Fire-King Chanticleer or Country Kitchen pattern, $25.00 – 28.00. Courtesy of www.randomretro.etsy.com

"Gay Rainbow Milk and Cream Pitchers," primary colors, Hazel-Atlas product premiums, $8.00 each.

Kellogg's advertisement, *Good Housekeeping*, 1946, $4.00.

Model J-408. About $4.00 a week after small down payment.

1950s advertisement, $4.00.

Curtain tie-backs, fruit, set of two,
$6.00 – 8.00. Courtesy of
www.antiquesonfarmington.com

Curtain tie-backs, teapots, set of
two, $6.00 – 8.00. Courtesy of
www.antiquesonfarmington.com

Glassware, Scotties, Deco style, assorted sizes and manufacturers, $10.00 – 12.00 each.

Step stool, metal, red and white, repainted, $65.00 – 75.00.

Cosco Utility Cart advertisement, $5.00.

Step stool, chrome and vinyl, $22.00 – 25.00.

Stool, metal, red, original decal, $25.00 – 40.00.

Mod Kitchen

1960s advertisement.

Coffee carafe, plastic, Made in West Germany by Emla, $30.00 – 36.00. Courtesy of www.ModishVintage.etsy.com

Coffee cups, daisy pattern, set of four, $24.00. Courtesy of Sharon Potts, www.kitschykoo.com

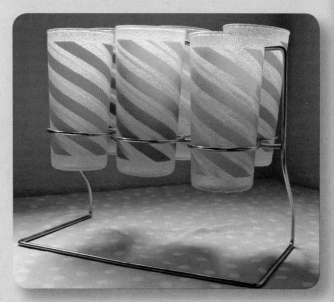

Beverage glasses in caddy, set of six pastel colors, candy stripe pattern, $30.00 – 36.00. Courtesy of www.ModishVintage.etsy.com

Flower Power

Canister, Ransburg, orange, blue butterfly, $8.00 – 12.00. Courtesy of Skilton Antiques, New Hartford, Connecticut.

Canister, Ransburg, orange, yellow butterfly, $8.00 – 12.00. Courtesy of Skilton Antiques, New Hartford, Connecticut.

Canister, "Flour Power," orange, white flowers, set of four, $30.00 – 36.00.

Mod canister set, set of four, orange, white with black polka dots, $36.00 – 40.00.

Dime-Store Housewares

Smiley Face bank, ceramic, McCoy, 1970s, $45.00 – 50.00. Courtesy of www.antiquesonfarmington.com

Wall clock, molded plastic, by New Haven, California, mid-1970s, $75.00. Courtesy of www.modhaus.com

Italian Toucan lamp by Ferrari, Milan, California, 1970s, $275.00. Courtesy of www.modhaus.com

Beverage glasses, unmarked, daisies, $6.00 each. Courtesy of www.DoNotDestroy.etsy.com

Enameled steel casserole by Cathrine Holm, Norway, California, 1960s, $65.00. Courtesy of www.modhaus.com

Dime-Store Housewares

Snack pagoda, $25.00 – 45.00.
Courtesy of Sharon Potts,
www.kitschykoo.com

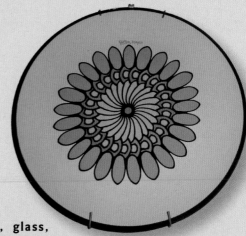

Plate, Peter Max, glass,
green, 1960s, $50.00 – $75.00.
Courtesy of www.DoNotDestroy.etsy.com

Plate, Peter Max, glass,
orange, 1960s, $50.00 – 75.00.
Courtesy of www.DoNotDestroy.etsy.com

Apron, terrycloth, vibrant flowers,
1960s, $10.00 – 15.00. Courtesy
of www.ModishVintage.etsy.com

Dime-Store Housewares

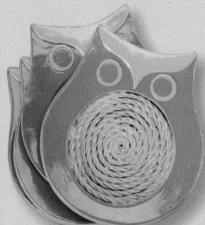

Coasters, owls,
set of four,
$12.00 – 15.00.

Canisters, plastic, flower design, set of four,
$24.00 – 30.00. Courtesy of
www.ImSoVintage.etsy.com

1960s advertisement.

Casserole, enameled steel, by Finel of Finland, circa
1960s, $60.00. Courtesy of www.modhaus.com

Canister set, green with bright red-orange
poppies, Ransburg, Indianapolis, $30.00 –
50.00. Courtesy of Heather Dietz,
www.LovethatVintage.com

At Sears . . exclusive patterns in fine quality imported
IRONSTONE

• An extra-strong ceramic fired at such high temperatures it becomes completely oven proof, detergent and craze resistant.
• Highly resistant also to chipping, cracking. Set a beautiful table with minimum upkeep. So _white_ contrast colors fairly sizzle. Japan.

Ironstone	45-piece Service for 8			54-piece Service for 8		
	Catalog Number	Shpg. wt.	Price	Catalog Number	Shpg. wt.	Price
(1) Federalist . . .				21 P 42385L	48 lbs.	$38.98
(3) Autumn Harvest . .				21 P 42625L	48 lbs.	32.98
(4) Clover				21 P 42635L	50 lbs.	32.98
(5) Blue Grapes				21 P 42655L	50 lbs.	34.98
(6) Tangerine . .				21 P 42645L	50 lbs.	34.98
(8) Moonstone . .				21 P 42537L	43 lbs.	28.98
(9) Tierra				21 P 42517L	40 lbs.	32.98
(10) Emerald Isle . .				21 P 42527L	40 lbs.	32.98
(12) Blue Bonnet . .	21 P 42706L	32 lbs.	$24.98			
(13) Del Mor† . .	21 P 42726L	35 lbs.	24.98			

†No. (13) Del Mor is a 47-piece Service for 8. It includes a 2-piece 8-cup Coffee Pot.

Sorry, patterns 2, 7 and 11 are not available.

See Open Stock and Composition Chart on opposite page

"Charge it" if you wish . see pages 435 and 436

CPBKM AEDGL | Sears | 849

Dime-Store Housewares

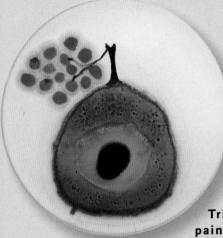

Cup and saucer set, Metlox Wild Poppy, 1970s, $15.00 – 45.00 per piece. Courtesy of www.modhaus.com

Trivet, Swedish glaze painted porcelain, circa 1970s, $75.00. Courtesy of www.modhaus.com

Tea set, porcelain with stylized floral transfer design, Made in Japan, circa mid-1960s, service for four, $45.00. Courtesy of www.modhaus.com

Stoneware dishes by Midwinter Stonehenge Pottery (UK), Sun pattern, circa 1970s. Pieces range from $10.00 – 25.00. Courtesy of www.modhaus.com

Teapot, creamer and sugar set, ceramic, "Wales, Made in Japan," green and purple, $40.00. Courtesy of www.DoNotDestroy.etsy.com

Dime-Store Housewares

Recipe box, tin, flowers, $12.00 – 15.00. Courtesy of www.ModishVintage.etsy.com

Recipe box, tin, flowers, Syndicate of Pennsylvania, $12.00 – 15.00. Courtesy of www.thebuttercup.etsy.com

Recipe box, tin, flowers, Syndicate of Pennsylvania, $12.00 – 15.00. Courtesy of www.thebuttercup.etsy.com

Placemats, quilted, orange, Sunflower yellow, 1970s, $22.00 – 24.00. Courtesy of Carin Brown, Mod-central.

Dime-Store Housewares

Coffee mugs, porcelain, Op Art design, Made in Japan for Holt-Howard, circa 1960s, set of four, $40.00. Courtesy of www.modhaus.com

Kitchen curtains, cotton, two panels, $18.00 – 25.00. Courtesy of www.ModishVintage.etsy.com

Tea towel, cotton, butterfly pattern, $8.00 – 12.00. Courtesy of www.ModishVintage.etsy.com

Coffee cup, $6.00 – 8.00. Courtesy of www.vintagegoodies.etsy.com

Coffee cups, $6.00 – 8.00 each. Courtesy of www.vintagegoodies.etsy.com

Colorful Era Cooking & Baking

**Porcelain Enamelware
Aluminum Ware
Mixers, Choppers, Grinders & Juicers
American Dinnerware
Stove & Range Accessories**

Young brides of the 1930s and 1940s would return from their honeymoons and take trips to their local variety stores to shop for household wares to "set up house." Today collectors scout out tag sales and flea markets looking for these very same appliances, pots and pans, ovenware pieces, tools, gadgets, and kitchen cooking and baking items. Nostalgia is in, and collectors of all ages enjoy replicating vintage looks in their homes today. In recent years, manufacturers of small appliances and kitchenwares have featured products with retro colors and designs that mimic those of the colorful era. Many collectors, however, want the real deal and are after the authentic versions of these desired and practical collectibles. One word of caution, however, is that older appliances may need to be rewired or refurbished before they are used. In some cases, you may need to keep them for display only. I found this out the hard way myself, when my favorite mixer wasn't working. I decided to save the day and try out a vintage mixer that was being stored in my garage. I plugged in this old fella and it started to smoke and spark. It was then that I ran to the supermarket and picked up a new Betty Crocker hand mixer!

If you would like to connect to experts, groups, and associations that specialize in small and large appliances as well as cooking and baking wares, try consulting *Maloney's Antiques & Collectibles Resource Directory.*

NOW! the NEW Sunbeam MIXMASTER
MODEL 10 AUTOMATIC
REG. U. S. PAT. OFF.

gives you all these advantages

The perfect gift for Mother's Day May 13

LIGHTER... HIGHER... FINER-TEXTURED CAKES !

More *EVEN* mixing and greater AERATION with these NEW, LARGER BOWL-FIT BEATERS

See how all the batter is carried into and through them—how their surfaces conform to the actual contours of the bowl. No piling up of dry ingredients on the outer edges. No unmixed whirlpools. No by-passed pockets. All the batter gets a thorough, even mixing in LESS TIME—*automatically.*

The larger outside BOWL-FIT beater is curved to fit the contour of the bowl all the way to the bottom. The larger inside BOWL-FIT beater is shaped to cover the flat bottom surface all the way to the center.

NEW, LARGER HEAT-RESISTANT BOWLS

Both bowls are now larger. The large bowl now holds 4 quarts for generous quantities of batter, potatoes for whipping, etc. The smaller bowl is now sufficiently large to whip 6 eggs for a double-meringue, etc.

Sunbeam Mixmaster does the perfect mixing job because the bowls revolve automatically. The new BOWL-FIT beaters are in correct relation to the bowl. ALL the mixture goes into and through them for EVEN mixing every time. Your hands are always FREE to add ingredients in correct proportion.

ORDINARY FOOD MIXER | *Sunbeam* **MIXMASTER**

Actual photograph of angel food cakes made in baking tests with ordinary food mixer and with the new Sunbeam. You can SEE and TASTE the difference when your food mixer is the new Model 10 Sunbeam Mixmaster.

Sunbeam advertisement, $8.00.

Porcelain Enamelware

Cookware and bakeware and other kitchen accessories for food preparation showed significant changes during the colorful eras. Food preparation, once a back-breaking task, would be lightened tremendously during the 1930s through the 1950s. The load was not only lessened by the development of more efficiently designed kitchens, but also of the introduction of cookware and bakeware that was significantly lighter in weight and easier to clean than the wares of previous generations — the cast-iron pots, kettles, and skillets that were used with coal or wood burning sources of heat. Enamelware had been around for decades in Europe and entered U.S. markets in the 1800s. Porcelain enamelware in this country was very popular, being advertised with slogans such as "clean as china." It remained a healthy industry until the arrival of shiny new aluminum pots and pans, which then became the household favorites.

Porcelain enamelware is made by applying a glass-like finish or coating to metal utensils using a high degree of heat. The term porcelain actually refers to a way of enameling or applying the coating, usually white to metal. Porcelain enamelware was usually found on kitchen tabletops, kitchenware, and advertising signs. Enamelware is smooth, nonporous, and easy to clean. Quality in enamelware depends on the number of coats of enamel and the thickness of the base. White enamelware usually has one dark base coat and two coats of the white surface color.

It is a little tricky to talk about new versus old enamelware. These terms can get confusing unless you use some demarcation date. In this book we are focusing on the colorful eras, which coincide with the great interest by manufacturers to bring color into kitchens. The enamelware industry was just beginning in the 1800s, but in the 1900s manufacturers wanted to come up with new ways of enameling and inventors held onto their secret enameling formulas dearly, introducing competing products regularly. Each generation saw improvements in enamelware, with a full range of products.

Early Enamelware

Early enamelware was heavier in weight than the pieces you will find associated with the "modern" kitchen of the dime-store era. These older products were generally gray or combinations of white and red or blue with patterns — described as swirls, spatter, and mottled, for example. There were indeed solid colors, such as white with black trim, but these pieces also tended to be heavier in weight and were apt to chip and stain more than the later pieces. In the 1900s competition was fierce, and as industry strides in technology and metallurgy developed even further, manufacturers eventually came up with enamelware that was stain resistant and almost chip-proof. Besides changes in weight, patterns, and enameling techniques, another way to distinguish products of different decades is by shapes, styles, handles, and hardware. These features changed between the 1800s and the 1900s. By looking at old magazine advertisements and catalogs you can get a good idea of how these products evolved over time.

Timeline

So on a timeline, earlier graniteware (1800s through early 1900s) is largely gray, red, or some shade of blue, with patterns. It is followed by later enamelware (1920s – 1950s), which was produced to coordinate with the kitchens of their periods. From the 1920s, when there was an interest in the "sanitized" kitchen that emphasized white surfaces and hospital-looking décor and products, you will find, lo and behold, lots of pieces of white or porcelain enamelware with black trim. These housewares did indeed look like they belonged in a sanatorium.

White & Red Trim Enamelware

Coffeepot, porcelain, white with red trim, $25.00 – 30.00.

Pots, porcelain, Fesco, original labels, white with red trim, graduated sizes, set of three, $25.00 – 28.00. Oven mitt shown, $6.00 – 8.00.

Double boiler, porcelain, white with red trim, $25.00 – 30.00.

Porcelain enamelware utility bucket by Fesco, white with red trim, $45.00 – 48.00.

Porcelain "enameledware" advertisement, $3.00 – 4.00.

CHOICE OF 4 COLORS
GREEN · IVORY · BLACK · RED

"EASY POUR" TEA KETTLES

DUETTE SAUCE PAN SETS

VAPOR SEAL DUTCH OVENS

6 CUP TEA POTS

FEDERAL DRIP COFFEE MAKERS

Again Federal Says
A NEW ONE *if it Chips*

Save cooking time and trouble, save food flavor and vitamins—
and save money . . . You can do it with Federal Chip-proofed
Stainless Guaranteed Enamelware, because these beautiful utensils
are unquestionably the most efficient and durable in the world . . .
and they're very much more sanitary and easier to clean. Remember
this ware provides vapor-seal Chromium Covers for healthful water-
less cooking, Bakelite Knobs and quick heat-conducting Black
Bottoms that save 20% to 40% on fuel. By actual tests it is 36
times more durable than ordinary enamelware.

INDIVIDUAL ITEMS AS LOW AS 95c
(Slightly higher in Far South and West)

See this line in lovely colors and new, convenient shapes
at your local Department, Hardware or Specialty Store or write . . .
Federal Enameling & Stamping Company, Pittsburgh, Pennsylvania. World's Largest Manufacturer of Enameled Kitchenware.

*Here is a new, con-
venient Strainer
Covered Sauce Pan
in brilliant Mirror
Black with Stainless
White Lining . . .
Another exclusive
Federal Item.*

FEDERAL
CHIP-PROOFED STAINLESS
GUARANTEED ✦ *ENAMELWARE*
* 36 TIMES MORE DURABLE BY ACTUAL TEST

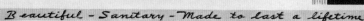

Beautiful - Sanitary - Made to last a lifetime

Federal enamelware advertisement, *American Home,* **1934, $8.00.**

The Colorful Eras

What is significant about the decades of the 1930s, 1940s, and 1950s is how enamelware began to show colorful changes. Porcelain enamelware began to come not only in white but also in color. But this look was different from that of the finishes of the very early pieces. Kitchenware, including enamelware pots, pans, and accessories, could match or coordinate with the prevailing color scheme of the times. This emphasis on décor and interior design was a new idea for homemakers. White and black enamelware hung around way after the 1920s, even when kitchens were changing. What can I say? Some folks still love white and black! When color entered the kitchen, the white and black pots and pans did indeed, however, have some company. Enamelware of the thirties would change to Depression green, cream, or combinations of these two colors with black, white, silver trim, or interior coatings. Cream with red trim was also available. Federal Enameling & Stamping Company made a chip-proof stainless line of enamelware with Bakelite knobs, which came in either red, green, or creamy yellow and was sold at hardware and specialty shops. Most homemakers during these years however, owned simpler, more basic lines of enamelware. The forties would see lots of white enamelware with red trim and the introduction of other colors as well. A 1945 industry advertisement proclaimed that "out of the war comes Porcelain on Steel Enamelware" that was "new and improved." Housewives could pick up enamelware at their local five and dimes and choose from many products such as double boilers, saucepans, teapots, coffeepots, basins, and other wares.

Baking & Cooking Time

During the colorful eras, kitchen tools and accessories often had wood or Bakelite handles and knobs in many colors, with red and yellow being very popular. Bakelite was the first man-made plastic and was discovered by a New York chemist named Leo Baekeland in 1907. Bakelite is the trade name for plastics produced by Bakelite Ltd. in England and Bakelite Corp. in America. The chemical name is a plastic called phenol formaldehyde (Phenolic). Kitchen collectors are always wondering whether they are buying items made of Bakelite or Catalin. Let me clear up the confusion. In 1927, the Bakelite patent expired and Bakelite was acquired by the Catalin Corporation, which then began mass producing Bakelite.

Bakelite is a strong thermoset plastic that does not burn, melt, or chip. Compared to wood, Bakelite kitchenwares were promoted as more hygienic and able to stand the heat of boiling and even sterilization. Kitchen gadgets, tableware, and accessories in the 1920s through the 1950s were available with Bakelite lids, tops, and parts. In the 1940s, chrome-plated electric kitchen appliances often had Bakelite handles. Today, chrome tea and coffee sets as well as barware with Bakelite handles and trim are very collectible. Older appliances such as Kenwood's 1948 electric mixer that featured black Bakelite knobs and fittings are collected with much interest for their innovative designs.

Made on Nantucket (www.madeonnantucket.com) has one of the largest collections of both jewelry and Bakelite kitchenwares you will ever see for sale in one place. It also hosts Bakelite collectors parties throughout the summer. Who knew that Bakelite, our first man-made plastic, would be adored for so many years by so many collectors?

Turquoise Enamelware

Coffeepot, complete, $24.00 – 28.00. Courtesy of Collinsville Antiques Company of New Hartford, Connecticut.

Saucepan set with rack, $32.00 – 36.00. Courtesy of Collinsville Antiques Company of New Hartford, Connecticut.

Frying pan, $15.00 – 18.00. Courtesy of Collinsville Antiques Company of New Hartford, Connecticut.

Covered casserole, drizzled white pattern lid, $24.00 – 26.00. Courtesy of Collinsville Antiques Company of New Hartford, Connecticut.

Pastel Enamelware

Teapot, porcelain, original label, Fesco, yellow with black wood and metal handle, $25.00 – 35.00.

Baking pan, yellow with black trim, white interior, no markings, $20.00 – 25.00.

Pots, yellow with black trim, white interior, graduated sizes, set of three, $18.00 – 25.00.

Pot, pink with black trim, hard-to-find color, $25.00 – 35.00.

S.O.S. advertisement, 1940, $8.00.

Aluminum Ware

Aluminum cookware, kitchenware, and giftware were abundant in the 1940s and 1950s because aluminum was used instead of other materials, which were reserved for the war effort. Aluminum is a lightweight metal that does not rust, is resistant to many forms of corrosion, and conducts heat well. Originally cast, aluminum was later rolled in sheets and became ideal for baking utensils such as cake and muffin tins, baking sheets, pie pans, and other lightweight kitchen tools and accessories. Skillets, saucepans, steamers, and stockpots can be made from sheet or cast aluminum. Aluminum cooking utensils have been around for quite some time, but the newer hammered and colored aluminum has brought increased attention to aluminum in recent years. The 1990s saw a whirlwind of interest in decorative and color-dyed aluminums by collectors who seemed to have gobbled up all the bride's gifts from earlier generations. In the 1960s, there was concern that there was a link between aluminum and Alzheimer's disease, especially when cooking with acidic food, but no evidence has supported this link.

Aluminum cookware was first introduced in the late 1800s, but it was not as popular with housewives as graniteware, which was less expensive and more reliable. Improvements in aluminum products would continue, and at the turn of the century, the Aluminum Cooking Utensil Company of New Kensington, Pennsylvania, introduced its trade name, Wear-Ever, to the market in 1903. Its lines were divided into two groups being sold either as retail or by canvassers who did home demonstrations. Aluminum continued to grow, and by 1924 there were dozens of companies, such as Wagner, Mirro, Alcoa, Club Aluminum Utensil Company, West Bend, and others manufacturing cast aluminum cookware. The Club Aluminum Utensil Company was the Pampered Chef Company of that era, selling its products home to home through something called the party plan. In a 1923 Club Aluminum recipe booklet the manufacturer states, "Aluminum products are sold direct to Home Managers Through Health Lecture Demonstrations, which are conducted in the home free of cost with no obligation."

In this section you will also find products made of stainless steel, which is virtually resistant to corrosion and not easily scratched or dented, but is a relatively poor heat conductor. Stainless steel is often used and preferred for flatware, serving pieces, accessories, and other kitchenwares, or combined with other materials when used for cooking. In 1937, Revere Copper & Brass introduced the first copper-clad-bottom stainless steel cookware, and in 1949, S. W. Farber Inc., of New York, promoted its aluminum-clad stainless steel pots and pans. In later decades, the focus would be on the interiors of cooking wares, with attention to nonstick surfaces, which gained popularity in the sixties.

S.O.S. advertisement, 1940s, $8.00.

Teapots & Coffeepots

A&P advertisement, $3.00 – 4.00.

KitchenAid coffee grinder, KitchenAid Electric Housewares Division, the Hobart Manufacturing Co., Troy, Ohio, $25.00 – 35.00.

Teapot, tea ball inset, aluminum, Universal, $18.00 – 25.00.

Coffee percolator, aluminum, stove top, Universal, $18.00 – 25.00.

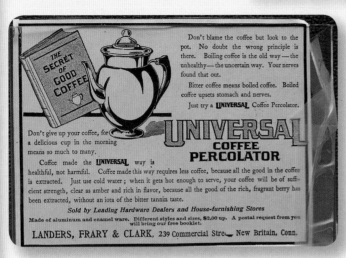

Advertisement, Universal coffee percolator, $6.00 – 8.00.

Coffee percolator, aluminum, stove top, Universal, $18.00 – 25.00.

Teapot, aluminum, Universal, $18.00 – 25.00.

Coffee percolator, aluminum, stove top, Universal, $18.00 – 25.00.

Coffeepot, aluminum, unmarked, $8.00 – 10.00.

Coffeepot, aluminum, Wear-Ever, $10.00 – 12.00.

Teakettle, aluminum, unmarked, $10.00 – 15.00.

PERCOLATORS			DRIP POTS		
4 cup		$3.25	4 cup		$3.75
6 cup		3.50	6 cup		4.25
8 cup		3.75	8 cup		4.50

Ask for prices on other sizes. They're at your favorite
department, hardware or housewares store NOW!

(All prices slightly higher in the West)

See WEAR-EVER on the ALCOA Program, "SEE IT NOW"
over the CBS-TV Network, every Sunday.

Friendly to Flavor
WEAR·EVER
Aluminum Coffee Makers

WEAR·EVER
T A C
ALUMINUM
U C O
TRADE MARK
REG. U.S. PAT. OFF.

© TACUCO 1952

THE ALUMINUM COOKING UTENSIL CO., DEPT. 5109, NEW KENSINGTON, PA.

109

Wear-Ever advertisement, 1950s, $6.00 – 8.00.

Wear-Ever New Method Cooking Instruction Book, booklet, 1939, full-color photos, includes recipes, product details, and cleaning instructions, $8.00 – 12.00.

Wear-Ever advertisement, $3.00 – 4.00.

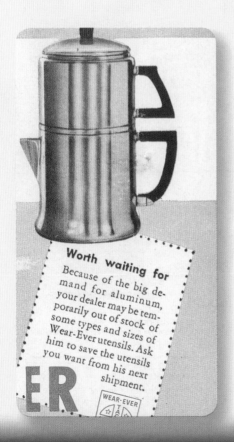

107

Mixers, Choppers, Grinders & Juicers

In recent years there has been a renewed interest by collectors in acquiring small kitchen appliances and gadgets. Some collectors just enjoy discovering unusual items, while others buy these items to go with their vintage and retro kitchens. Although this book centers on the decades of the 1930s, 1940s, and 1950s, I would like to offer some background on mixers, choppers, and grinders, which were familiar accessories in the dime-store era.

In 1910, entrepreneur Fred Osius of Racine, Wisconsin, and mechanically gifted Chester A. Hamilton formed the Hamilton Beach Manufacturing Company, which launched commercially used mixers for malts and shakes. Soon the home market would be tapped and Hamilton Beach would introduce the first cake batter mixer. Other companies, such as A.F. Dormeyer and A.C. Gilbert, a New Haven company known for the popular Erector construction sets, joined in the making of appliances. Gilbert came up with the Polar Club hand mixer, which could detach from its stand, as well as many other models. A 1930 magazine advertisement featured a Polar Club mixer made "expressly for the Wesson Oil–Snowdrift people" that sold for $11.95 and gave you "fluffy mayonnaise, feathery popovers, velvety cakes, tender waffles, whipped cream and loads of other dainties."

But the leader of tabletop electric mixer companies was the Sunbeam Corporation, which thrilled housewives everywhere with the development of the now-famous Mixmaster in 1931. This all-in-one product came in different models, with numerous attachments that could shred, slice, chop, whip, peel, and grind foods as well as open cans, sharpen knives, and even juice oranges and lemons. Sunbeam's mixer cost less than the competing Hobart Manufacturing Company's KitchenAid model. Sunbeam was heavily promoted and was indeed a big success. Collectors will find many Sunbeam products, as well as product information and recipe booklets available.

When buying electric mixers, be sure the basic parts such as the bowls and beaters are included and are of course the matching parts. Bowls of glass, metal, or milk glass usually come in a set of two, with one larger than the other. I have often seen different manufacturers' bowls being been substituted for the originals. Take a good look at them and check for chips or cracks. It is also very important to check that the beaters are present and that they do indeed belong to the mixer you are buying. Try them out before you bring the mixer home, to make sure they fit properly.

You may not always be able to find all of the attachments, but remember that prices should reflect age, rarity, and how complete the mixer is. I have included Universal's food and meat chopper, which was available way before the colorful eras but was still a popular item for many households and amazingly stayed around for a very long time.

Homemakers in the colorful eras used a variety of gadgets and devices in the home kitchen to make cooking preparation easier. Of course the electric mixer, which was indeed the earliest version of today's food processor, was a welcome addition to the home. But, like folks today, many cooks relied at times on their hand-held mixers and choppers, which were able to whip up some "dainties" without too much fuss.

Coffee, tea, and chocolate were brought to America at the end of the seventeenth century, and there have been endless ways to grind coffee beans with models that mount on the wall, tabletop, and even laptop, with a variety of metal, wood, and iron cases and glass reservoirs to hold the beans. In the early 1900s, grocery stores as well as specialty coffee and tea shops would grind coffee as a service for their customers. But in 1937, an electric coffee grinder was available for household use, offered by the KitchenAid division of Hobart Manufacturing Company of Troy, Ohio. It sold for $12.75, and today this appliance and similar ones are of great interest to many collectors who enjoy finding unique early appliances.

Electric mixer, Universal, excellent condition, complete, 1940s, $65.00 – 75.00.

There's Nothing Like It!

It has no clamp!

THE NEW

UNIVERSAL

TAB-L-TOP

Food Chopper

Out of the cupboard—and a TAB-L-TOP Chopper is ready to use! There's no clamp to fuss with. Rests snugly on counter or table's edge. And for effortless cleaning ease, body of chopper swings apart. Only $5.95 at your Universal dealer's.

FREE BUDGET-STRETCHING RECIPES

Write Virginia Woods — Landers, Frary & Clark, 502 Center Street, New Britain, Connecticut, for exciting and tasty chopped meat and vegetable recipes.

No Clamp! No Fuss! No Bother!

Swings Apart to Clean in a Jiffy!

UNIVERSAL

LANDERS, FRARY & CLARK, NEW BRITAIN, CONN.

Universal advertisement, $3.00.

Sunbeam Mixmaster advertisement, *Better Homes and Gardens*, 1940, $3.00.

Speed & Whipper two-cup glass reservoir with red and white plastic lid, $12.00 – 15.00.

Nut grinder, japanned top, glass reservoir, $12.00 – 15.00.

Tab-L-Top Food
and Meat Chopper,
Universal, 1950s,
$15.00 – 22.00.

Sunbeam Mixmaster with juicer attachment,
1940s, missing large mixing bowl. As shown,
$25.00; complete, $35.00 – 45.00.

Electric mixer, Universal, 1930s,
fair condition, $30.00 – 35.00.

Universal Food & Meat
Chopper, box with full contents,
Landers, Frary & Clark Co., New
Britain, Connecticut,
$10.00 – 15.00.

Sunbeam Mixmaster recipe and instruction booklet, copyright 1950, red cover, Sunbeam Corporation, Chicago, Illinois, $6.00 – 8.00.

Sunbeam Mixmaster recipe and instruction booklet, orange cover, Sunbeam Corporation, Chicago, Illinois, $6.00 – 8.00.

Sunbeam Mixmaster advertisement, Woman's Home Companion, December 1940, $3.00 – 4.00.

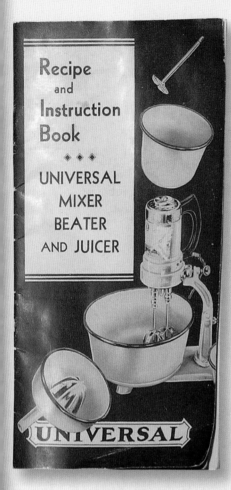

Recipe booklet, Universal, $6.00 – 8.00.

90

"LOOKS LIKE CHRISTMAS IS HERE TO STAY!"

UNIVERSAL Christmas Gifts "Make a Merry Christmas last the Whole Year Through"

UNIVERSAL'S NEW GLIDER is unique among irons. Air-cooled ports in the super-deck construction protect hands from heat radiation. Other features are finger-tip heat control which also cuts off current and wrinkle-proof round heel. $7.95

UNIVERSAL WAFFLE MAKER in new "Coronet" pattern, is built close to the table for easier serving, yet table-top is always cool. Heat indicator shows when to pour batter. Tray is extra wide. Chromium plated with "Platina" panel. $6.95

THIS UNIVERSAL TURN-EASY TOASTER is second to none in styling. Pattern is "Coronet"—newest and smartest. Opening bread rack turns the toast. Mirror-bright chromium finish with "Platina" panel and black bakelite trimmings. $3.95

MULTI-SPEED CONTROL with full power at every speed! UNIVERSAL Mixer's new direct drive does away with costly power unit for heavy tasks. Dial the speed you want according to easily-read markings. With Juicer Attachment. $23.75

WOMEN WHO OWN a New UNIVERSAL Mixablend claim it's one appliance that's never on the shelf. It has so many uses. Adds new health foods to your menu. Blends many delicious beverages. Whips, beats, mixes, purees and chops. $19.95

Christmas starts at your UNIVERSAL Dealer's. See him today.

UNIVERSAL
THE TRADE MARK KNOWN IN EVERY HOME
LANDERS, FRARY & CLARK, New Britain, Conn.

Woman's Home Companion   December 1940

Juicer, Universal, $15.00 – 22.00.

Universal Christmas advertisement, *Woman's Home Companion*, December 1940, $6.00 – 8.00.

Recipe and instruction booklet for Hamilton Beach Model K food mixer, $8.00.

Appliances advertisement, *Woman's Home Companion*, 1940, $8.00.

KitchenAid Model 3C mixer, attachments not shown, 1950s, KitchenAid Electric Housewares Divison, the Hobart Manufacturing Co., Troy, Ohio, $25.00 – 35.00.

77

Electric cooking is so simple and safe, my little girl cooks on our new Norge Electric Range

See the new 1942

NORGE
ELECTRIC RANGES

Model E-450

7 Sparkling models

Electric cookery is safe, clean, cool and healthful with the new 1942 Norge Electric Ranges . . . 6 different heats on every top unit give you a cooking speed for every need . . . new balanced-heat oven with beautiful, easy-to-clean, light gray porcelain lining, is automatically controlled for perfect baking and roasting . . . new one-piece top and sloping backrail for greater beauty and convenience. See these beautiful, newest electric ranges . . . at your Norge dealer's now.

Model E-350

PRICES START AT
$99⁹⁵
AT THE FACTORY

NORGE DIVISION BORG-WARNER CORPORATION, DETROIT, MICH.

NORGE
ROLLATOR REFRIGERATION • ELECTRIC RANGES • GAS RANGES
WASHERS • WATER HEATERS • HOME HEATERS
COMMERCIAL REFRIGERATION

Model E-300

See NORGE *before you buy!*

Woman's Home Companion June 1941

Norge Electric Ranges advertisement, *Woman's Home Companion*, June 1941, $6.00.

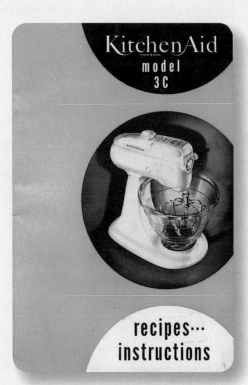

KitchenAid
model
3C

recipes...
instructions

Recipe and instruction booklet for KitchenAid Model 3C, KitchenAid Electric Housewares Division, the Hobart Manufacturing Co., Troy, Ohio, $6.00 – 8.00.

American Dinnerware

The American Dinnerware industry started in Ohio and was quite active in the late 1930s and the 1940s. Many manufacturers offered sets of their products in patterns or lines. These makers offered dinnerware, ovenware, and accessories. Imports were common and mimicked the styles of the American manufacturers.

Families in the 1930s, 1940s, and 1950s liked having everyday dishes with coordinating ovenware and accessories, which were made of earthenware and were typically very colorful. Homer Laughlin's Fiesta, Harlequin, and Riviera lines were cheerful additions to the colorful era kitchens. Harlequin was made exclusively for Woolworth's, and Riviera was made for the G.C. Murphy Company in 1938.

As early as the 1930s, pottery companies also made dinnerware and serving pieces in white or off-white, with bold designs and patterns with special decals added. Many of these kitchenwares were used from oven to tabletop. Homer Laughlin called these lines OvenServe and Kitchen Kraft. Homer Laughlin not only made Fiesta, but like many companies in those years, produced many successful ovenware lines in addition to its dinnerware. I am partial to the ovenware lines that have colorful decals of flowers or "stepping flowerpots" with Art Deco influence and red or blue border trim, made by Laughlin and others. Other collectors are fond of Homer Laughlin's Mexicana themes, which are very hot right now and going for mucho dinero ("much money"). Harker's Red Apple decal and Knowles's pear and apple motif are also popular among collectors. Of all the dinnerware and ovenware pieces you are likely to find today, Universal's Cattail is by far the most common pattern you will come across. It is therefore possible to pick up these collectibles at more reasonable prices than it is some of the other patterns made by Universal and similar companies.

In the pages that follow, you will see dinnerware and ovenware accessories that feature the flower decals and fit quite well into this category, Fabulous Flowers. You can see how nice all these flower-themed pieces look together when they form collections. For easy reference I have grouped them together by their manufacturers. Some of the manufacturers you will see in this section are Pottery Guild, the Harker Pottery Company, Homer Laughlin, Edwin M. Knowles, as well as pieces made in Japan and unknown pieces.

The American Dinnerware collection shown on pages 116 – 127 is from the private collection of Kathy Hotchkiss. Kathy has also contributed information about identification and values of items.

Casserole with two-handled lid, Universal Potteries, Inc., marked Oven Proof, floral design, $30.00 – 45.00.

Covered casserole, Universal Potteries, Inc., Bittersweet pattern, Camwood Ivory shape, $30.00 – 45.00.

Prices in the Good Ole Days

If you want to have some fun, take a look at the advertisements for dinnerware and ovenware in old mail-order catalogs such as those put out by Montgomery Ward or Sears. In 1939, Montgomery Ward sold a three-piece Pottery Guild waffle or batter set for $1.98. Expect to pay $45.00 – 65.00 for the same set today. A three-piece Pottery Guild bowl set sold for $1.19 in 1939, and one bowl might fetch $25.00 – 30.00 today. Here are some more comparisons. If you were buying dinnerware to sell in your shop in the 1930s, you could buy a dozen five-piece mixing bowl sets for $28.00, the value of one mixing bowl in today's market. If you wanted to feature salad sets to match the other dinnerware lines you sold, you could order one dozen three-piece sets, which included the fork, spoon, and bowl, for $15.00. In the 1930s and 1940s, you could by an entire dinnerware set plus several accompanying serving pieces for what one plate might cost at Pottery Barn today.

Common Defects

When collecting these pieces, which can easily be well over 60 or 70 years old, one would expect them to show signs of aging and wear. I reject many pieces that have yellow or brown discoloration on the outside or interior surfaces or heavy crazing. Crazing is the small network of tiny cracks that occurs over time and suggests that moisture or heat has gotten under the glaze.

I bought a larger version of the "fish-wave" Deco creamer shown on page 10, which appeared to be in good condition but was very dirty. So, I began to run the creamer under water to rinse off surface dirt, and boy was I in for a surprise. Once I removed the creamer from the water, this lovely treasure I had found turned into an ugly, brown, crazed, and unappealing white elephant ready for the junk pile. I placed it on a shelf in the basement and forgot about it for awhile. Weeks later, the creamer was looking much better after it had dried out, but not quite as promising as it looked the day I bought it. Crazing is considered to be a defect, and many collectors pass up pieces that are crazed. I should mention that sometimes a manufacturer has added crazing as part of the design of the piece. This is an intentional look and is referred to as a "crackle" or "craquelle" finish.

Sometimes a collector will come across a piece that doesn't come along very easily but has a small defect such as a tiny chip under the lid. Many collectors will accept a defect if they are interested in adding this piece to their collection but are not concerned about resale or using the piece. Price, of course, should reflect this imperfection and be considerably lowered.

Cracks are a different issue. Cracks migrate or spread and are not a good sign. I have, however, bought bowls with small cracks inside at very fair prices when I am only interested in keeping them as shelf pieces or have a particular use in mind for them. One huge mixing bowl I found with a small interior crack sits on my kitchen counter holding the week's packages of bread and rolls. A damaged teapot I own was salvaged and used to hold pens and pencils near my kitchen phone.

Decals and "Red-Liners"

Most of the ovenware items that I present have decals as well as some painted lines or trim. In pottery plants, hundreds of pottery pieces would be pushed on carts, to be "red-lined" by "liners" who painted the decorative red color lines on dinnerware. These liners were paid pennies for trimming a dozen pieces. Decals are decorations or designs such as flowers or fruits that are printed on a special type of paper that may have a plastic coating. This graphic is then positioned onto the ceramic piece with a special mixture, called sizing, and baked in the kiln. Once this process is complete, the decal or decoration is permanently part of the glaze. Decal companies sold the same decal to many different potteries. Some decals, however, were exclusive to a particular manufacturer. Before decals, back in the eighteenth century, designs were added by transfer printing. This method was much more involved and requried an engraving plate, oily ceramic pigment, and several firings.

When buying ovenware and accessories with designs, be sure the color on the decoration as well as the painted rings on the rim are bright and bold and not faded. Pay close attention to these concerns when purchasing an item on eBay or other online auctions, when you cannot handle the item in person. If the seller does not include this information in the description, ask for details. You might as well be clear about all the possible defects that I have mentioned thus far, such as discoloration, crazing, chips, cracks, and color fading. There are other special points about these collectibles that are worth mentioning. I have grouped these tips according to types of products:

Batter Sets versus Tea or Coffee Sets

Dishes and their matching accessories such as teapots, batter sets, casseroles, salad sets, serving wares, and even scales were very colorful and were often found in mail-order catalogs, dime stores, and department stores. Batter sets are often confused with tea sets, which they are not. A batter set consists of a pitcher for the waffle or pancake batter, a syrup pitcher, and a tray. These sets became popular when the electric waffle maker was in vogue and homemakers could make waffles or pancakes at the kitchen table instead of at the stove. I often see sellers on eBay promoting what they think is a tea set or coffee set or parts of these kitchenwares instead of their true identity as batter sets.

Casseroles versus Covered Bowls

There is a distinction between a casserole and a covered bowl. Casseroles generally have deep grooves that the lids sit atop. Covered bowls generally do not have such indentations. If you find a dish with a groove, it probably had a matching cover, and I'd proceed with caution when buying this incomplete item. On the other hand, it is very common to find bowls that came with and without covers. Many times manufacturers sold sets of three to five bowls as well as single pieces with and without covers. So when it comes to bowls there has to be more flexibility, because there were so many products and special promotions by these companies.

Canisters and Refrigerator "Bowls"

Canister sets or refrigerator "bowls" were ceramic in the 1930s and 1940s before they were replaced by plastic varieties postwar. They generally came in graduated sizes that stacked. These storage pieces can be found in rounded bowl shapes or in more cylindrical styles. Canisters, moreso than refrigerator dishes, generally should have three pieces and matching covers.

Sometimes collectors believe the pieces without covers are flowerpots, which they probably are not. I have bought canister sets that are not complete, using the piece that is missing its top as a handy container for odds and ends, while the covered dishes are used to hide my chocolate.

Refrigerator Jugs

Refrigerator pitchers or jugs were used to chill water or other beverages. One of these should almost always have a corked plug that fits snugly into the spout. As you can imagine, many of these pieces, which have been around for such a long time, have corks that are broken apart or missing altogether. Know what you are buying and remember that the price should reflect the condition and completeness of the collectible you are interested in purchasing.

Reproductions

Although you may come across retro/vintage-look kitchenwares that are newly made to look like the old pieces, I am not overly concerned about reproductions in this area of collectibles. When I do discover look-alikes, they generally have bar codes on the bottoms of the pieces or are stamped "dishwasher safe" or "microwave safe," sure clues that they are not the originals.

General Electric "Roast-of-the-Month" club advertisement, $6.00.

Oval platter, unmarked, $18.00 – 24.00; covered bowl, marked Bake Oven, $16.00 – 24.00; small plate, unmarked, $6.00 – 8.00.

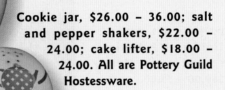

Cookie jar, $26.00 – 36.00; salt and pepper shakers, $22.00 – 24.00; cake lifter, $18.00 – 24.00. All are Pottery Guild Hostessware.

Cookie jar, unmarked, fruit design, $35.00 – 45.00.

Coffee server, Knowles Utility Ware, Mexican design, $35.00 – 50.00.

Tom and Jerry set with 12 cups, Universal Potteries, Inc., red and ivory, Upico shape, $60.00 – 75.00.

Refrigerator jug, Universal Potteries, Inc., red and blue floral design, $30.00 – 45.00.

Refrigerator jug, unmarked, floral design, $30.00 – 45.00.

A STARTLING STATEMENT TO WOMEN!

You can be a Better Cook! Serve better-tasting meals—more easily, more economically than ever— with a new General Electric Range

Teapot, Universal Potteries, Inc., Calico Fruit pattern, Camwood Ivory shape, $30.00 – 40.00.

Teapot, Universal Potteries, Inc., Garden Glory pattern, Upico Ivory shape, $30.00 – 40.00.

Butter dish, unmarked, Garden Glory pattern, Camwood Ivory shape, $30.00 – 40.00.

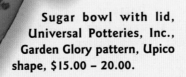

Sugar bowl with lid, Universal Potteries, Inc., Garden Glory pattern, Upico shape, $15.00 – 20.00.

Water pitcher with lid, Oven Proof by Pottery Guild, colorful flower design, $35.00 – 45.00.

Plate, marked Wheelock Peoria, windmill scene, $15.00 – 20.00.

Pitcher and custard cup, Knowles Utility Ware, pastel fruit design, pitcher, $24.00 – 32.00; custard, $7.00 – 10.00.

Platter and pitcher, Hostessware by Pottery Guild, colorful stylized fruit with polka-dot leaves design, platter, $18.00 – 24.00; pitcher, $24.00 – 32.00.

Salt and pepper, unmarked, floral with teakettle design, $18.00 – 22.00.

Salt and pepper, unmarked, Mexican design with fruit on reverse side, $18.00 – 22.00.

Salt and pepper, unmarked, Kitchen Bouquet pattern, $18.00 – 22.00.

Salt and pepper, unmarked, Southwestern pottery design, $18.00 – 22.00.

His mother made grand shortcake!

"Bob kept raving about his mother's old-fashioned biscuit shortcakes. I was scared stiff at the thought of making any. But now Bisquick has been my salvation," says Mrs. R. W. Burmeister, Happ Road, Northbrook, Ill.

Men do go rapturous over old-time rich biscuit shortcake. And, being Mrs. 1942, you are in luck! You simply add cream and sugar to Bisquick . . . for shortcake that completely enslaves the man in your life.

Flaky, rich, warm, . . . heaped with crimson juicy berries. Of course he raves. Bisquick makes that kind of shortcake! Six home-type ingredients are skilfully blended in Bisquick:

Pure vegetable shortening, baking powder, Gold Medal Flour, salt, sugar, powdered milk. Try Bisquick. It's tested by Betty Crocker staff.

Free! Our new "Daily Menu and Shopping List". Helpful pad — each sheet gives space for day's menus, also lists staple groceries. Check needs, then take sheet to store. To get your pad, mail postcard to Betty Crocker, Dept. 1810, Minneapolis, Minn., by July 15, 1942.

Just add cream and   sugar to Bisquick

Bisquick advertisement, 1940s, $6.00 – 8.00.

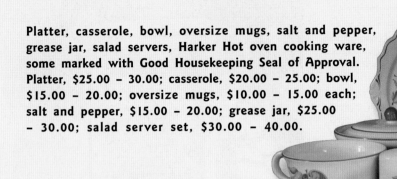

Platter, casserole, bowl, oversize mugs, salt and pepper, grease jar, salad servers, Harker Hot oven cooking ware, some marked with Good Housekeeping Seal of Approval. Platter, $25.00 – 30.00; casserole, $20.00 – 25.00; bowl, $15.00 – 20.00; oversize mugs, $10.00 – 15.00 each; salt and pepper, $15.00 – 20.00; grease jar, $25.00 – 30.00; salad server set, $30.00 – 40.00.

Bowl and cups, all unmarked, Little Jack Horner, Hickory Dickory Dock, and Tom Tom the Piper's Son designs, $10.00 – 15.00 each.

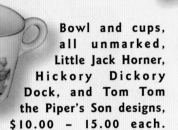

Cookie jar, $24.00 – 36.00; pitchers, $18.00 – 24.00; All are Pantry Bak-In Ware, Petit Point House pattern.

Casserole with lid, OvenServe, Wildflower design, $25.00 – 35.00.

Frigidaire advertisement, $8.00.

Casserole dishes with lids, and bowl, Pantry Bak-In Ware by Crooksville, Petit Point House pattern, $24.00 – 30.00 each.

Cake lifters, center one is Calico Ribbon pattern by Harker, others unmarked, $18.00 – 24.00 each.

Large pitcher, $26.00 – 36.00; small pitcher, $18.00 – 20.00; custards, $6.00 – 8.00 each. Univeral Potteries, Inc., Circus pattern, Upico shape, ivory and blue.

Plate, Knowles, cowboy roping calf design, $8.00 – 12.00

Bowl, Oven Proof Bak-Serv, Good Housekeeping Seal of Approval, Hollyhock and Fence design, $24.00 – 26.00.

Bean pot, Pantry Bak-In Ware by Crooksville, Cottage by the Shore design, missing lid, $20.00 – 30.00.

"Let's go in and see what's new!"

There's nothing like GAS for

BROILING

Gas gives you the intense heat needed to brown meats so fast that loss of juices is prevented. Full flavor is saved.

ROASTING

Gas gives you the oven ventilation which produces crisp, juicy roasts. Excess moisture is allowed to escape, preventing that flat "steamed" flavor.

BAKING

Baking requires an unlimited range of oven temperatures evenly distributed. That's why Gas assures light, evenly browned cakes, pies and breads.

FRYING

Perfect, speedy frying requires instant high heat—even spread of heat under the skillet—numberless heat variations. Gas gives them all!

BOILING

Faster! Gas brings foods to a boil in ⅔ or less the time of other fuels. Because it is more flexible, it gives you the exact degrees of heat you need.

Gas advertisement, 1940s, $8.00.

Stove & Range Accessories

The 1930s through 1950s period brought significant changes in the way foods were cooked and kept warm. Gone were the days of kettles and large pots on open fires in smoky, dark, small kitchens. Gas and electric stoves and ranges were continuously upgraded, with manufacturing companies competing for business. Instruction booklets with accompanying recipes were widely distributed to help the homemaker learn about all these new appliances and styles of cooking. Booklets from the 1930s are generally priced a little higher than those from later decades, especially if they have covers with Art Deco designs or unique full-color graphics. Booklets which feature products that describe models, parts, and care instructions can be found for a few dollars more than booklets that only contain recipes.

American Gas Association

In the 1940s and early 1950s, the American Gas Association (AGA) flooded magazines with advertisements touting the benefits of gas as "the wonderful fuel for cooking." During the war years, its advertisements also included a reminder for Americans to buy United States savings bonds and stamps. Many of the AGA advertisements also featured husbands and wives explaining the benefits of using gas, each explaining his or her side of the story. The wife's side was, "I'm the one that is going to use this range... so it's got to be fast." The husband replied, "I'm the one who has to pay the bills for food and fuel...so the economy and efficiency make sense to me." Roles of women and men were clearly defined during the colorful eras and were boldly promoted in home magazines. Women were at the helm of their kitchens and homes, and men were responsible for the finances, decisions, and buying products that "we'll be proud to show our friends."

Ranges

A look through vintage magazines during the colorful eras, especially the 1940s, shows numerous advertisements for gas and electric ranges all promoting their appliances as being energy efficient, faster, modern, and beautiful. Manufacturers appealed to busy homemakers by promising them sparkling, easy-to-clean, safe, healthful appliances. Dozens of companies competed for customers and became household names. Manufacturers of ranges included Roper, Norge, Magic Chef, Frigidaire, Caloric, General Electric, and others. A 1942 Norge electric range promotion pictures a mother and daughter cooking, and the caption reads, "Electric cooking is so simple and safe, my little girl cooks on our new Norge Electric range."

I have presented company advertisements to show you the variety of styles, models, and advertising themes that were prevalent during these years.

Cake saver, tin, green, $15.00 – 18.00.

Ohio Blue Tip Matches, box with full contents, the Ohio Match Co., Wadsworth, Ohio, $4.00 – 6.00.

YOU CAN LOOK   TO KELVINATOR

New! KELVINATOR Electric Ranges
with Amazing HEAT-UP SPEED!

Get Cooking Heat in Seconds!

Now, Kelvinator makes electric cooking better than ever . . . with *new heat-up speed!* The "Rocket" Unit on the new Kelvinator Electric Ranges heats up in seconds! New radiant heat broilers get red hot in *ten seconds!* New giant oven preheats to 350°F. in *less* than 5 minutes!

And What Wonderful Results!

With that brilliant new "Automatic Cook" double oven Kelvinator, you can bake and broil at the same time! Roast the largest turkey you'll ever want to serve! Bake six pies, eight loaves of bread, or all four layers of a cake at one time, in one oven, with *no* shifting of pans! Cook applesauce with *no* water . . . custards without scorching, in an ordinary pan. *Cook full oven meals automatically.*

Completely New Design!

Imagine having automatic cooking, big double ovens, new heat-up speed, and Kelvinator's exclusive "Colormatic" Controls . . . all in today's most beautiful electric range! Now that all this can be yours, together with the time-proved advantages of electric cooking, why put up any longer with less modern cookery methods? See the new Kelvinators at your Kelvinator Dealer's.

Better Baking! You'll get amazing results with the controlled heat in Kelvinator's big double ovens. Delicious pies, cakes, cookies, bread . . . full meals . . . with the same enviable results . . . every time!

"AUTOMATIC COOK"! Put full meals in the oven . . . set Kelvinator's "Automatic Cook" control . . . and take afternoons off! Perk your morning coffee while you sleep! Here's really carefree cooking!

"COLORMATIC" CONTROLS! New! Jewelled lights flash the heats you dial. 7 brilliant colors for 7 different heats . . . each exactly the same *measured* heat . . . every time you dial it! And uniform results—always!

TUNE IN! *"Star of the Family."* Kelvinator TV show starring Morton Downey, on CBS Network. See your local paper for time and station.

LOOK FOR THIS EMBLEM. Awarded to "5-Star" salesmen of Kelvinator Dealers, it assures you the highest standard of courteous, helpful service.

Get More . . . *Get*

Kelvinator electric range advertisement, $8.00.

Platter, Harker
Pottery Company,
$25.00 – 30.00.

1941 Frigidaire Electric Ranges

give you more for your money
Inside and Out!

1. Brilliant New Beauty! New concepts of range beauty, created by a world-famous designer, include ultra-modern fluorescent lighting.

2. More Useful—Faster! Exclusive advantages assure cooler, cleaner, more carefree cooking. New Radiantube cooking units are 18% faster!

3. Use Less Current! Lowest cooking cost in Frigidaire history. Exclusive new Radiantube units 15% more efficient. Exclusive oven improvements give additional savings on current.

4. Sensational New Values! Many brilliant models. Every one an outstanding bargain value inside and out!

Exclusive advantages in the new Frigidaire Ranges assure you cooked foods that taste better, look better, and retain vitamins better.
From top lamp to base—inside and out—General Motors and Frigidaire have packed each range with brilliant, convenient improvements. Pictured above is the beautiful, new Frigidaire Electric Range Model B-60.
Don't fail to see your Frigidaire Dealer today!

FASTER HEAT · LESS COST

NEW! Radiantube Cooking Units! *Exclusive Frigidaire Feature!* 18% faster, 15% more efficient than any previous models. All have five practical heats to meet every cooking need!

8 Models from which to choose

✳ **IMPORTANT!** All prices quoted are Dayton, Ohio, delivered prices. Transportation, Special wiring, State, Federal and local taxes (if any) extra. **All Prices Subject to Change Without Notice.** See Your Frigidaire Dealer for Local Prices.

Baking! Roasting! Broiling! *Full-size Even-Heat Oven!* Twin heating units, Evenizer and Simplimatic Oven Control create such perfectly regulated temperatures everywhere in the oven that novices bake and roast like experts. Adjustable shelves and automatic oven light add to convenience. Thick insulation saves current; keeps kitchen cooler.

B-10 SENSATIONAL BARGAIN	B-15 PACKED WITH FEATURES	B-45 A DE LUXE VALUE	B-60 MODEL ILLUSTRATED
$104.75*	$129.75*	$165.00*	$199.75*

Frigidaire Division, General Motors Sales Corp., Dayton, Ohio. Canadian Factory at Toronto

Frigidaire Electric Range

Value to match Frigidaire Refrigerator

Frigidaire electric range advertisement, 1941,
$6.00 – 8.00.

Match holder, handcrafted,
sometimes referred to as
a wood cutout, probably
1930s or earlier, hard to
find, $25.00 – 45.00.

37 years "My wife's a good cook," says the Rev. V. D. Ruch, Council Bluffs, Ia., "and after 12 years abroad—cooking with other fuels—she says nothing compares with her new Gas range for better cooking, better flavor, and economy. It cooks best by *every* test!"

18 years "Budgets are more important today than ever before in our years together," says Mrs. Donald P. Robinson, New Haven, Conn., "so it's wonderful that meat-shrinkage in the oven of my automatic Gas range amounts practically to nothing!"

1 year "I've kept my job—and I keep house, too, thanks to my automatic Gas range," says Mrs. Sulo W. Korpi, St. Clair Shores, Mich. "I set the automatic clock-control, go off to work, and we come home to a perfectly cooked, complete oven dinner!"

"we love our new automatic Gas ranges!

This glamorous step-saving New Freedom Gas Kitchen® deserves the very last word in automatic cooking appliances — and here it is! A brand-new **TAPPAN** Gas range — just one of the many wonderful all-automatic ranges built to "CP" standards. They cook your dinner by clock-control while you're busy elsewhere. They're cool and clean — and easy to *keep* clean because of their beautiful modern design. For speed, economy, and superb cooking results — you simply cannot find anything finer. NO WONDER MILLIONS MORE WOMEN BUY MODERN GAS RANGES THAN ANY OTHER KIND. Go see these marvels in the **Spring Style Show** of automatic Gas ranges . . . at your Gas company or appliance dealer's . . . today!

AMERICAN GAS ASSOCIATION

 **GAS** cooks best by every test!"

®A.G.A.,INC.

Gas — the modern fuel for automatic cooking . . . refrigeration . . . water-heating . . . house-heating . . . air-conditioning . . . clothes-drying . . . incineration

American Gas Association advertisement, *McCall's*, 1952, $8.00.

1940s – 1950s kitchen illustration, $6.00 – 8.00.

1940s – 1950s kitchen illustration, $6.00 – 8.00.

Asweco box, replacement wicks, fits all burners, Asbestos Weaving Co., Gleasondale, Massachusetts, $8.00 – 10.00.

Booklets

Each of the range instruction and recipe booklets shown in this section are valued at $6.00 – 12.00. The majority of booklets shown are from the New Britain Industrial Museum, New Britain, Connecticut, collection of Universal products and advertising materials (www.nbim.org).

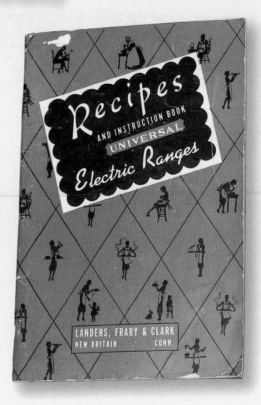

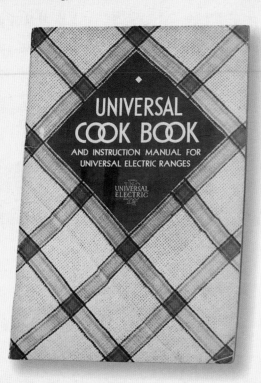

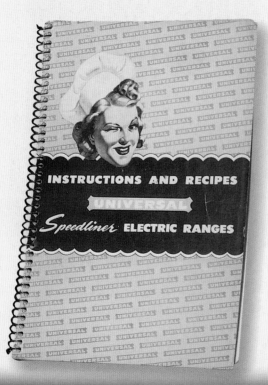

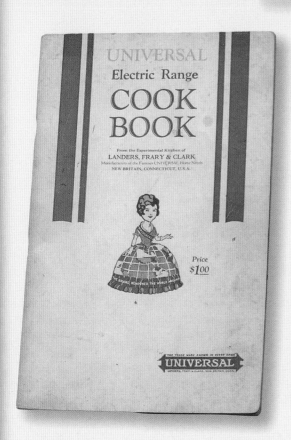

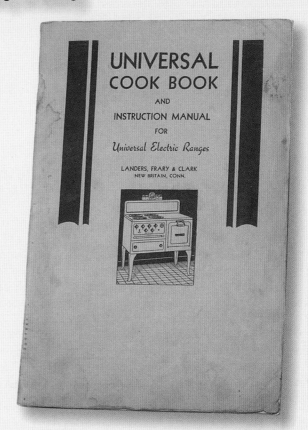

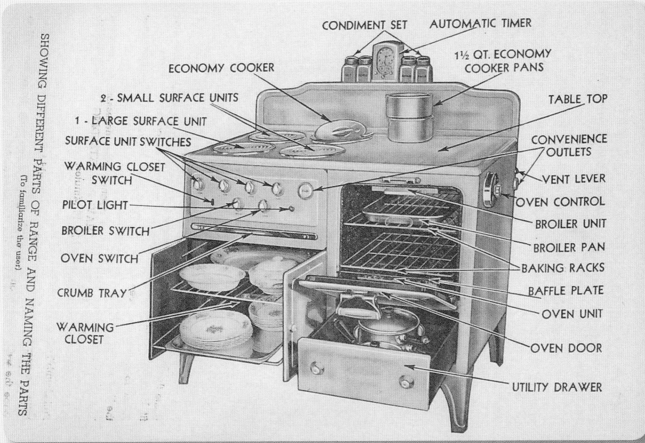

SHOWING DIFFERENT PARTS OF RANGE AND NAMING THE PARTS
(To familiarize the user)

CONDIMENT SET
AUTOMATIC TIMER
ECONOMY COOKER
1½ QT. ECONOMY COOKER PANS
2 - SMALL SURFACE UNITS
1 - LARGE SURFACE UNIT
SURFACE UNIT SWITCHES
WARMING CLOSET SWITCH
PILOT LIGHT
BROILER SWITCH
OVEN SWITCH
CRUMB TRAY
WARMING CLOSET
TABLE TOP
CONVENIENCE OUTLETS
VENT LEVER
OVEN CONTROL
BROILER UNIT
BROILER PAN
BAKING RACKS
BAFFLE PLATE
OVEN UNIT
OVEN DOOR
UTILITY DRAWER

Chef Themes
Black Americana
The Piggy Pals
Dutch Treat
Charming Couples
Bottlecap Figures & Chalkware

During the colorful eras, families would venture down to their favorite Woolworth's or five and dime and find lots of ceramic planters, salt and pepper shakers, figurines, wall décor, and trinkets that they could bring home for pocket change. Many of the collectibles you will see in this section once sat on a shelf at Woolworth's or were brought home by tourists as inexpensive souvenirs. The majority of these ceramics and novelties are imports and in their day were attractively priced. Today these collectibles can easily sell for up to 50 to 100 times higher than their original prices.

I like finding novelty items with their original paper or foil labels in place. Sellers often remove original labels or cover up the prices and other markings. The logic was that if the seller disguised the fact that the item was a "cheap" import, it might sell for more money. In today's marketplace, however, leaving the original markings in place helps to date items and does not necessarily work against the seller. Collectibles with Made in Japan or Occupied Japan stamps and labels have gained a large audience.

The chef themed collectibles on pages 137 – 145 are from the private collection of Marianne Dow of www.msdowantiques.com

Chef Themes

Salt & pepper shakers,
ceramic, marked Japan,
$10.00 – 15.00.

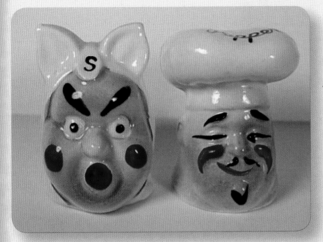

Salt & pepper shakers,
ceramic, marked Japan,
$10.00 – 15.00.

GE advertisement, 1950s, $8.00.

15-cubic-foot
REFRIGERATOR-FREEZER

Wall pocket with three hanging small spice shakers, incomplete, $12.00 – 15.00. Complete set with four shakers, $30.00 – 45.00.

Spice shaker set of six with wooden rack, ceramic, $20.00 – 25.00.

Cookie jar, McCoy Pottery, $50.00 – 75.00.

Grease jar, small, $24.00 – 32.00.

Cookie jar, Pierre Chef, Red Wing, blue, $75.00 – 100.00.

Cookie jar, American Bisque, $50.00 – 75.00.

Vintage pink kitchen illustration, 1950s.

Salt & pepper shakers, $12.00 – 15.00.

Spoon rest, ceramic, $12.00 – 15.00.

**Jello molds, plastic, yellow, white, or red,
$18.00 – 24.00 each.**

**Notepad holder, plastic, red,
$12.00 – 15.00.**

**Notepad holder, plastic,
aqua, $10.00 – 12.00.**

Spoon rests, plastic, assorted colors, $8.00 – 10.00 each.

Reamer/cutter, plastic, red,
$8.00 – 10.00.

Notepad holder, plastic,
$12.00 – 15.00.

Wall décor, pot holder,
$18.00 – 22.00.

Notepad holder, plastic, red and
white, $15.00 – 20.00.

Salt and pepper shakers with chef figurine, red and white shakers, $18.00 – 22.00.

Salt and Pepper shakers, plastic, $12.00 – 15.00.

Grocery list maker, plastic, Noma, as shown without pegs and faded print, $12.00 – 15.00. Complete and very good condition, $25.00.

Back view of previous photo.

143

Pillsbury advertisement, 1946.

Black Americana

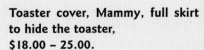

Toaster cover, Mammy, full skirt to hide the toaster, $18.00 – 25.00.

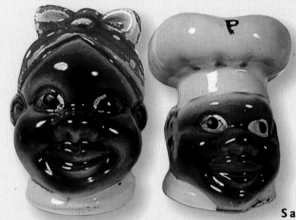

Salt and pepper shakers, Mammy, ceramic, Japan, $18.00 – 24.00.

Wall décor, pot holder, Mammy, $18.00 – 25.00.

Notepad holder, plastic, Aunt Jemima premium, $18.00 – 25.00.

The Piggy Pals

Collectors love pigs. Anything pig is collected, whether it be salt and pepper shakers, planters, banks, figurines, books, or textiles; you name it, if it is pig related, it is hot! Maybe collectors know what farmers already know, that pigs are much smarter than the public thinks. In fact, the pig is one of the smartest animals in the barnyard and not the sloppy lazy character it is made out to be. In parts of the world, pigs are used as "watch dogs." In the French countryside, in Alba, Italy, and in other regions around the globe, the large female pigs are raised to sniff out truffles, a food delicacy similar to mushrooms. I am not talking chocolate here, I am talking the original use of the term truffle, which refers to a fungus. Since the times of the Greeks and Romans, truffles have been used in Europe as delicacies, as aphrodisiacs, and as medicines. How does $250 to $450 per pound sound to you for a little indulgence? Even pigs know the difference between Godiva chocolate and mushrooms, and that is why the pig is used for this job. The female pig becomes excited when she sniffs a chemical that is similar to the male swine sex attractant. The problem is, pigs like eating truffles, and often dogs are used to dig the ground. Who knew pigs had such interesting occupations when out of the barnyard?

Besides sniffing for truffles, pigs have held other highly esteemed roles in history, especially in Hollywood films and children's literature. Porky Pig debuted during the colorful eras as a 1936 cartoon character for Warner Brothers, along with his pal Daffy Duck. A decade earlier, Piglet was becoming adored as Winnie-the-Pooh's friend. Before Piglet, Wilbur was the pig that was saved from being turned into bacon by Charlotte, a spider in the book *Charlotte's Web* by E.B. White. Oh, and what about the Three Little Pigs, who have been around in published versions of this fairy tale since the eighteenth century and gained popularity in a 1933 Walt Disney animated cartoon? Indeed, pigs have had a colorful past and continue to be stars even in current times, with the ever-so-popular Miss Piggy, Babe, and others.

Before concluding my little background discussion of pigs, I should mention the origin of the piggy bank. During the fifteenth century, people placed a variety of items in dishes made of orange pygg clay. In the eighteenth century coins would be placed in these dishes, referred to as "pygg dishes." Then jars were used and called "pig banks" in Europe. Pig banks became "piggy banks." It was customary to believe that pigs brought luck and good fortune, and piggy banks were often given as gifts.

Pigs in every generation are adored and collected, and not just by children, but by adults as well. In fact, you would be surprised at how many adults have come into my shop and simply melted when they have found other sets of cute piggies to add to their collections. All of the pigs that are presented here are ceramic and unmarked. Many of them resemble pigs made by Shawnee, Royal Copley, and others, but these cuties have no maker indicated and are not referenced as such. Often in these decades, many manufacturers copied each other, and imports abound. All of these planters and figurines are valued at $15.00 – 26.00. Pigs are easy to sell and tend to be priced a little higher than similar ceramics, because they have a big audience.

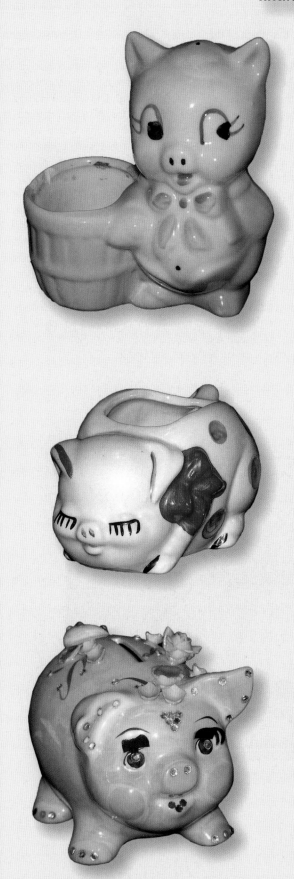

Dutch Treat

Dutch-related symbols such as wooden shoes, windmills, tulips, boys and girls in traditional dress, landscapes, and more were popular additions to the kitchenwares and textiles of the colorful eras, especially during the 1940s. I was very curious about how these design features made their way into the popular culture of the times. I will share with you what I have learned, and I invite you to update me further if you have other ideas on this subject.

During these decades there was an increase in travel to Holland, and travelers returned home to America chronicling their trips with articles and photographs in American magazines. Slowly, Americans would get to know "Dutchness" by seeing distinctive symbols of Holland such as windmills, clogs, tulips, landscapes, children, and designs in the photographs being brought home by tourists. But why, I still wondered, did we see more Dutch stereotypes in the 1940s? Rick Erickson, the author of *Royal Delft: A Guide to De Porceleyne Fles*, explained further:

"The American 'Roaring Twenties' was an optimistic period, with emphasis on new technology, daring attitudes, and modern styling. But much of that changed with the Great Depression (and the related problems such as crop failure, the dust bowls, and so on). That is when the Americans seem to have started looking for folksy, homespun, almost old-fashioned motifs for decoration, in retreat to the security of home, family and 'Old World' Holland." He added that the Porceleyne Fles factory was represented at the 1937 World's Fair in New York. bringing Dutch designs into America. He also mentioned that there were other Dutch-American connections, such as the large settlement of Dutch families in New York.

Remember too that Roosevelt was of Dutch extraction and was in the White House during this time period. Also, Holland was neutral during both world wars and was considered "safe," easily identified as comfortable "old world." The Dutch motifs became, if not fashionable, at least popular. One final important point that I will add is that many people associated fine craftsmanship with the goods that came from Europe and thought highly of products that came from Germany, Austria, and Holland. It makes sense that American manufacturers would want to continue this image of artisan-level workmanship here in America by using Dutch symbols on kitchenwares and textiles.

Figurines, Dutch couple kissing, $15.00 – 18.00.

Figurine, Dutch gentleman, probably part of a pair, 7½"; single, $10.00 – 12.00.

Salt and pepper shakers, Dutch couple, ceramic, 2" high, $10.00 – 12.00.

Figurines, Dutch couple, originally priced at 50¢, 1950, $12.00 – 15.00.

Wall hangings, Dutch boy and girl, chalkware, 4½", $15.00 – 18.00.

Figurines, Dutch couple, ceramic, Japan stamp, 6" high, $12.00 – 15.00.

Figurines, Dutch couple, ceramic, no markings, $18.00 – 24.00.

Charming Couples

Planter, ceramic, Gay Nineties couple, marked "3723c," red, black, and white, $9.00 – 12.00.

Music box, hard plastic base, celluloid children who kiss with movement, $20.00 – 25.00.

Salt and pepper shakers, plastic Gay Nineties couple shakers driving in old car, $18.00 – 22.00.

Figurines, bench sitters, blue and white young couple, has the look of California Pottery but is unmarked and likely an import, $20.00 – 25.00.

Bottlecap Figures & Chalkware

Bottlecap figures can be men or women and are a form of assemblage or folk art in which odds and ends are added to a figure made from old bottlecaps. On eBay they are generally listed under the category "Bottlecap Man." Characteristically, these figures hold a bowl in front of a wood block that serves as the torso. Metal, plastic, or colored aluminum or another material is often used for the bowl, which might hold a snack such as popcorn, nuts, or chips. Sometimes the bottlecaps are sprayed a color, and other times they are left in their original forms, showing the vintage of the caps used. During these decades, these handmade art forms, which had been around for ages, incorporated the popular images, personalities, and advertising icons of the 1940s and 1950s. Doesn't the bottlecap man shown on this page remind you of the 1951 United Fruit Company Chiquita Banana advertising icon (which seems to resemble the character of the very popular 1940s Brazilian movie actress Carmen Miranda)?

Many bottlecap figures appear to show other influences as well. Earlier bottle figures can have a folk art feeling or may be a bit more primitive looking, with nose rings, large dangling earrings, and painted faces on dark-stained wood tones suggestive of an African tribal look. I have also seen many bottlecap figures that are similar to the one shown on this page and are outfitted like Carmen Miranda but seem to have faces portraying the black Americana "mammy" ethnic stereotype, which appeared on many kitchen advertising products, kitchenwares, and textiles of the 1940s.

Wall hanging, fruit theme, chalkware, $15.00 – 18.00.

Wall hanging, fruit theme, chalkware, $15.00 – 18.00.

Bottlecap figure with fruit bowl as hat, $25.00 – 30.00.

Welcome to a

NEVAMAR®-*topped Table*

DINETTE BY

Lloyd

Write to Lloyd Mfg. Co., Menominee, Mich., for the store in your city showing this dinette.

NATCOLITE
NEVAMAR®
TABLE TOP

This table top is designed for lifetime beauty and service. In lasting colors, the surface will resist scratches, dents or ring-marks. It is not affected by alcohol, fruit acids or alkalies. It is resistant to cigarette burns and will withstand boiling water. Clean with a damp cloth. Washing with mild soap and warm water is permissible but seldom necessary.

Guaranteed by Good Housekeeping

THE NATCOLITE COMPANY
BALTIMORE, MD.

Come into a room that sings a cheering welcome! Sit down to a table that boasts a NEVAMAR top in true, clear decorator colors and eye-delighting patterns. A NEVAMAR top is so easy to live with . . . endures long wear, never needs care. Stains disappear with a swish of a damp cloth. See NEVAMAR-topped tables at your furniture or department store. America's leading manufacturers choose them because they bring lifetime service and lasting beauty into your home.

THE NATCOLITE COMPANY
Division of National Store Fixture Co., Inc. Baltimore, Maryland.

Makers of Lifetime Tables, Booths and Counters for the Restaurant, School and Hotel

GREY HAREWOOD

SAND OAK

MOTHER-OF-PEARL

Nevamar table top advertisement, 1950s, $8.00.

Dry Goods & Everyday Linens

**Aprons
Bottlecap Hot Pads
Pot Holders & Dish Towels
Hot Pads
Tablecloths
Card Party**

Collecting dry goods of the 1930s, 1940s, and 1950s is very popular at this time. In fact, you can see how much fun this hobby is when you join the gals and guys who are devoted members of the Vintage Tablecloth Lover's Club (www.vintagetableclothsclub.com).

In this section on dry goods, I will share with you many household items that were popular during the colorful eras and are sought after by today's collectors. The dime-store era was a time when color entered the home and homemakers were busy buying everyday linens and accessories to go with wall coverings, window treatments, and furnishings.

Fabrics, tablecloths, and kitchen textiles were vibrant, whimsical, and easier to care for than in earlier times. I remember as a child accompanying my parents to Woolworth's to buy oilcloth, which my dad would later use to line shelves or re-cover the chrome chairs in our kitchen. While Dad waited for the salesperson to measure out his oilcloth, Mom picked out new toaster and mixer covers, white plastic with black poodles. The covers are long gone, but the electric mixer is still cranking out great sponge cake.

Colorful era illustration, $6.00 – 8.00.

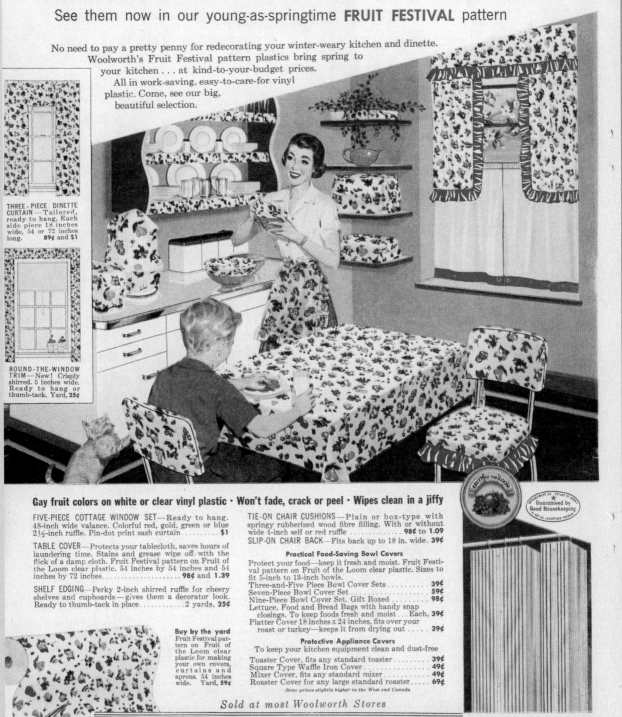

You can have a dream kitchen...at Woolworth's thrifty prices...with

Woolworth's PLASTIC ENSEMBLES

See them now in our young-as-springtime **FRUIT FESTIVAL** pattern

No need to pay a pretty penny for redecorating your winter-weary kitchen and dinette. Woolworth's Fruit Festival pattern plastics bring spring to your kitchen . . . at kind-to-your-budget prices. All in work-saving, easy-to-care-for vinyl plastic. Come, see our big, beautiful selection.

THREE-PIECE DINETTE CURTAIN—Tailored, ready to hang. Each side piece 18 inches wide, 54 or 72 inches long. **89¢ and $1**

ROUND-THE-WINDOW TRIM—New! Crisply shirred, 5 inches wide. Ready to hang or thumb-tack. Yard, **25¢**

Gay fruit colors on white or clear vinyl plastic · Won't fade, crack or peel · Wipes clean in a jiffy

FIVE-PIECE COTTAGE WINDOW SET—Ready to hang. 48-inch wide valance. Colorful red, gold, green or blue 2½-inch ruffle. Pin-dot print sash curtain **$1**

TABLE COVER—Protects your tablecloth, saves hours of laundering time. Stains and grease wipe off with the flick of a damp cloth. Fruit Festival pattern on Fruit of the Loom clear plastic. 54 inches by 54 inches and 54 inches by 72 inches . . . . **98¢ and 1.39**

SHELF EDGING—Perky 2-inch shirred ruffle for cheery shelves and cupboards—gives them a decorator look. Ready to thumb-tack in place . . . . 2 yards, **25¢**

Buy by the yard
Fruit Festival pattern on Fruit of the Loom clear plastic for making your own covers, curtains and aprons. 54 inches wide. Yard, **59¢**

TIE-ON CHAIR CUSHIONS—Plain or box-type with springy rubberized wood fibre filling. With or without wide 4-inch self or red ruffle . . . . **98¢ to 1.09**
SLIP-ON CHAIR BACK—Fits back up to 18 in. wide. **39¢**

Practical Food-Saving Bowl Covers
Protect your food—keep it fresh and moist. Fruit Festival pattern on Fruit of the Loom clear plastic. Sizes to fit 5-inch to 13-inch bowls.
Three-and-Five Piece Bowl Cover Sets . . . . **39¢**
Seven-Piece Bowl Cover Set . . . . **59¢**
Nine-Piece Bowl Cover Set, Gift Boxed . . . . **98¢**
Lettuce, Food and Bread Bags with handy snap closings. To keep foods fresh and moist . . . Each, **39¢**
Platter Cover 18 inches x 24 inches, fits over your roast or turkey—keeps it from drying out . . . . . **39¢**

Protective Appliance Covers
To keep your kitchen equipment clean and dust-free
Toaster Cover, fits any standard toaster . . . . **39¢**
Square Type Waffle Iron Cover . . . . **49¢**
Mixer Cover, fits any standard mixer . . . . **49¢**
Roaster Cover for any large standard roaster . . . . . **69¢**
Some prices slightly higher in the West and Canada

Guaranteed by Good Housekeeping

Sold at most Woolworth Stores

F. W. WOOLWORTH CO.

GARMENT BAGS—Fruit of the Loom vinyl plastic for a smart closet. To keep clothes neat and dust-free. Hold 8 or 16 garments. Zipper opening. 57 inches long. **2.19 and 2.29**

Woolworth's advertisement, 1951, $8.00.

WHY NOT GIVE AN APRON ?

IT IS a prize package in itself—pattern 1225. That's because it contains the pieces for three aprons, each one as smart as the smartest dress in your closet. Make them up for your friends and they will bless you for thinking of "just the right gift." Make them up for yourself and you will be ready for any doorbell.

The lines of version A (left) pulled in at the waist and gathered through the skirt, its big pockets, its touches of embroidery and its soft lavender chambray all add up to a high fashion mark. With version B (center) it's the low waistline look, the scalloped edgings, the pockets and the polkadots. With C (right), the ruffled shoulders and rickrack.

1225 Aprons. Sizes, 32 to 48 bust measure. Size 36 requires 2½ yards of 35-inch material for embroidered version: 1⅞ yards of 35-inch material with 11¾ yards bias binding for scalloped version: 2½ yards of 35-inch material with 5¾ yards rickrack braid for ruffled version. The price is 25 cents.

DRAWINGS BY RUTH MANLUAL

Companion-Butterick patterns may be bought from your local Butterick dealer or Woman's Home Companion, P. 8, Service Bureau, 250 Park Avenue, New York

Advertisement, "Why Not Give an Apron?" *Woman's Home Companion*, 1940.

Aprons

Three aprons, cotton, pinafore style, blue calico print, mint, $15.00 – 18.00 each.

Cotton, pastel print with terry-cloth pocket, $10.00 – 12.00.

Apron-making kit, pink, $6.00 – 8.00.

QUAKER CEREALS OFFER YOU HIGH-FASHION PATTERNS!

...exclusive originals by *Luis Estévez*
International award-winning designer

Free McCall's Apron Pattern in these packages

Here's a petite party fashion to tie around your waist! It's fun to make from the simple one-piece pattern now packed inside Quaker Cereal packages—and so easy, you can even make it by hand. Buy your favorite cereal. Make your pretty apron, soon!

If your store does not yet have the pattern packages, you can get your free apron pattern, anyway! Just send name, address and boxtop from any Quaker Cereal to: McCall Corp., Box 986, Dayton 1, Ohio.

Create your own exciting Wardrobe!

Your choice of 3 specially-designed McCall's Dress Patterns

(A) Wide-collared sheath with fringed bow at neckline. Fly-front, short unmounted sleeves, shapely lines, wide belt. Flattering for any time. Sizes 12-20; 40-42.

(B) Open-work triangular cutouts follow V neckline on bodice of subtly curved sheath. Short unmounted sleeves. Will make a lovely "basic black." Sizes 12-20.

(C) An over-sized cowl collar is stunning detail of slim, sleeveless sheath. Belts at natural waistline. Cool and trim for summer. Sizes 9-15; 10-16.

Just send box top and **25¢**

See order blank on packages

Apron advertisement, *McCall's,* 1950s.

Cotton, pinafore style, pink and black, mint, $15.00 – 18.00.

Cotton, pinafore style, turquoise and black; mint, $15.00 – 18.00.

Sheer, half style, pink and black, $10.00 – 12.00.

Sheer, half style, yellow and black, $10.00 – 12.00.

Bottlecap Hot Pads

Crocheted bottlecap hot pads are valued at $12.00 – 15.00 each. Courtesy of www.thebuttercup.etsy.com

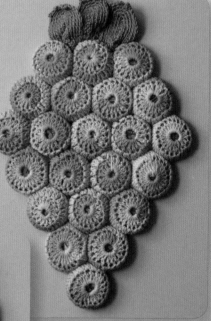

Pot Holders & Dish Towels

Pot holder, crocheted, blue with pink trim, $6.00 – 8.00.

Pot holder, crocheted, blue and white with red center, $6.00 – 8.00.

Pot holder, white with blue polka dots, set of three, $8.00 – 10.00.

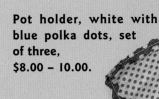

Booklet, *Pot Holders to the Rescue*, $8.00 – 10.00.

Pot holder, cro-
cheted, red and white,
$6.00 – 8.00.

Booklet, *Pot Holders*, instructions, $8.00 – 10.00.

Pot holder, unusual, hand crocheted,
white with yellow lemon ornament,
$12.00 – 15.00.

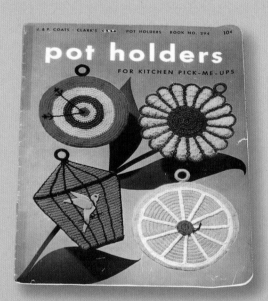

Booklet, *Pot Holders: For
Kitchen Pick-Me-Ups*, instructions, $8.00 – 10.00.

Hot Pads

Booklet, *Hot Plate Mats,* instructions, $8.00 – 10.00.

Hot pad, yellow and red ruffles, $8.00.

Hot pad or pot holder, red and white ruffles, $8.00.

Pot holder, green, yellow, and white ruffles, $6.00 – 8.00.

Dry Goods & Everyday Linens

Embroidered pot holders, $6.00 –
8.00 each; dish towels, $4.00 – 6.00
each.

Dry Goods & Everyday Linens

Crocheted pot holders shown on this page are valued at
$6.00 – 8.00 each. Courtesy of www.cottagerags.com

Tablecloths

Tablecloths shown on pages 166 – 175 are courtesy of The Little Round Table, www.happenstancestuffhappens.blogspot.com

Cotton, geometric checks with tropical foliage, $26.00 – 28.00.

Cotton, turquoise with grid pattern covered with nasturtiums. $36.00 – 46.00.

Cotton, chocolate brown grid with gold floral and kitchen pots, $36.00 – 42.00.

Heavy cotton blend, peach pink center grid, with multi-colored floral surround, Simplex with sewn-in label. $28.00 – 36.00.

Rayon, red poppies on lime and yellow large checked center, $36.00 – 42.00.

Cotton, red/white geometric with stylized leaves with metallic accents, Victory K & B "Leaves," circa 1950s, $28.00 – 38.00.

Rayon, green and gold pine cones with foliage, California Hand Prints, name is "Pacific Pine," sewn-in tag, $23.00 – 26.00.

Cotton, tropical foliage in a variety of colorways, $32.00 – 36.00.

Cotton/rayon blend, green version of "Fiesta Children," Calaprint sewn-in tag, $36.00 – 42.00.

Cotton, chicken wire with stylized fruit and flowers, California Hand Prints sewn-in tag, $42.00 – 52.00.

ABOVE: No. 1916 INSULATED TABLE PAD. Fits any shape table, resists heat, water, alcohol. 52x90 . . . . . 2³/₅ Books

(A) FLORAL PRINT TABLECLOTHS. Guaranteed fast colors and washable.

No. 1900 53x53. Gold . . . . ⁴/₅ Book
No. 1902 53x53. Red . . . . ⁴/₅ Book
No. 1904 53x53. Green . . . . ⁴/₅ Book
No. 1906 53x70. Gold . . . . 1¹/₅ Books
No. 1908 53x70. Red . . . . 1¹/₅ Books
No. 1910 53x70. Green . . . . 1¹/₅ Books

(B) No. 1912 SCRANTON LACE TABLECLOTH. Beauty in fine lace. Boxed for gift giving. 70x90 . . . . 1⁴/₅ Books

(C) No. 1914 DAMASK SET. 50x66 with 6 napkins, cotton & rayon . . . . 1¹/₅ Books

(D) No. 1898 FLANNEL BACK PLASTIC CLOTH. 52x52.
. . . . ⁴/₅ Book

(E) No. 1890 BLUE, 1892 RED CANNON PLAID DISH TOWELS. 6 for . . . . ⁴/₅ Book

(F) No. 1894 CANNON STRIPED DISH TOWELS. 6 for ⁴/₅ Bk.

(G) No. 1888 CANNON TERRY DISH TOWELS. 6 for 1 Book

(H) No. 1896 PRINTED TERRY DISH TOWELS. 6 for ⁴/₅ Book

Glamor in textiles

(J) No. 1998 FOAM RUBBER THROW PILLOW. Round solid foam rubber with zippered cover. Each . . . . 1¹/₅ Books
(K) No. 2000 TOSS PILLOW, COTTON FILLED. 15x15. Each . . . . ²/₅ Book
(L) No. 2002 FOAM RUBBER SQUARE PILLOW. With zippered cover of excellent quality . . . . 1¹/₅ Books
(M) No. 5736 HAND HOOKED RUG. Imported. Ideal for child's room. 1³/₅ Books

DISTINCTIVE THROW RUGS FOR EVERY ROOM IN THE HOME. LATEX NON-SKID BACKS — GUARANTEED WASHABLE IN ASSORTED COLORS.

(N) LOOP RUG. 24x48.
No. 1934 Red No. 1936 Green
No. 1938 Sandalwood . . . . 1 Book
(P) VISCOSE TWEED RUG. 24x36.
No. 1940 Red No. 1942 Hunter Green
No. 1944 Sandalwood . . . . 1 Book
(R) SCULPTURED VISCOSE RUNNER. 24x70.
No. 1946 Hunter Green No. 1948 Sandalwood . . 2 Books
(S) KEY EMBOSSED RUG. 24x36.
No. 1950 White No. 1952 Pink
No. 1954 Sandalwood . . . . ⁴/₅ Book
KEY EMBOSSED RUG. 27x48.
No. 1956 White No. 1958 Pink
No. 1960 Sandalwood . . . . 1¹/₅ Books

1950s catalog advertisement, $6.00.

Cotton, tropical foliage on bamboo grid, "Leacock Quality Hand Prints, Mandalay," paper tag, $26.00 – 28.00.

Rayon, black, red, and white geometric floral, Dunmoy sewn-in tag, $26.00 – 36.00.

Cotton, green and red plaid with small flowers, Startex sewn-in tag, $26.00 – 32.00.

Heavy cotton, golden yellow center grid with border of multicolored nasturtiums, $26.00 – 28.00.

Rayon blend, pink ground with floral wreaths, Leacock Prints sewn-in tag, "Cornwall," circa 1946, $24.00 – 26.00.

Styled in Paris

Blue, turquoise, and orange, stylized leaves, cotton blend, "Styled in Paris" printed on cloth, $42.00 – 52.00.

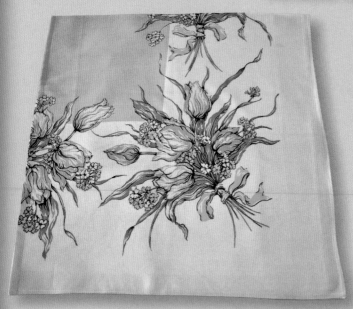

Spun rayon and cotton, golden yellow center, with tulip bouquets, paper tag reads "Leaspun Prints by Leacock, Kate Greenaway Series," Avon, hand printed, $24.00 – 26.00.

Rayon blend, brown ground with lime green plants, printed on the cloth is "Elling Design," $28.00 – 32.00.

Cotton, turquoise center and border, floral sprays, $36.00 – 42.00.

Cotton, red, white, and green floral, $28.00 – 36.00.

Rayon blend, floral with gold mesh design,
$34.00 – 42.00.

Cotton, seamist green with multicolored stylized floral,
Startex sewn-in tag, $36.00 – 42.00.

173

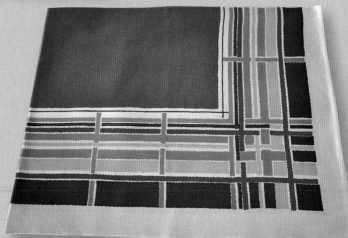

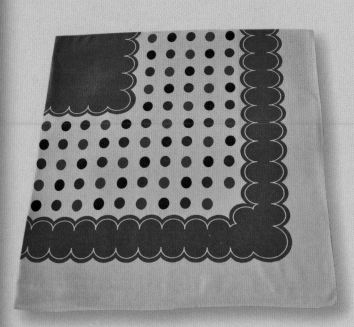

Cotton, green and red plaid with small flowers, Startex sewn-in tag, $26.00 – 32.00.

Cotton, red and black polka dots, red center and border, $36.00 – 42.00.

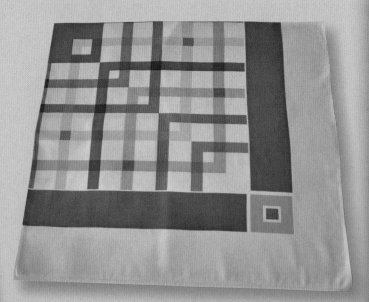

Cotton blend, solid blue border, with multicolored center grid, $26.00 – 36.00.

Cotton, green squares in different shades, small fruit and floral border, Startex sewn-in tag, $26.00 – 36.00.

Cotton blend, large plums on off-white background, Fairfield Linens, $26.00 – 28.00.

Linen, blue tropical leaves, stylized cherries on white ground, $26.00 – 36.00.

Cotton, yellow ground, white center, rimmed with pomegranate fruits and foliage, $26.00 – 28.00.

Rayon, speckled and lime green squares in center with colorful fruit border, Simtex sewn-in tag, $42.00 – 52.00.

Amazingly Tough Surface of New

SAMSON SUPER-TOP TABLE

WITHSTANDS HARDEST USE—EASY TO KEEP CLEAN

SUPER-TOP TABLE

$9⁹⁵

Matching Chairs, each............$ 5.95
Five-Piece Super-Top Set..........33.75
Deluxe Five-Piece Set............49.75
(Vinyl Upholstery—Spring Cushion Seats)

1. Spilled Drinks! No need to worry when the table is Super-Top! Spilled liquids wipe up easily and leave the table top unmarked!

2. Spilled Ink! Super-Top resists practically every type of stain. Just a whisk of a damp cloth and—presto—stains disappear like magic!

3. Hot Dishes! Super-Top's tough, damage-resisting surface won't scorch or mark when piping-hot dishes—even casseroles—are set right down on it!

IN ADDITION TO FOLDING FURNITURE FOR THE HOME, SAMSON ALSO OFFERS FOLDING CHAIRS FOR PUBLIC SEATING—FAMOUS FOR STRENGTH, BEAUTY, ECONOMY!

Used By Schools and Churches Everywhere!

"How To Save Money On Public Seating" is the title of a new booklet that is yours for the asking. Write us on your letterhead. See your Samson public seating distributor for special low prices on quantity purchases of Samson Chairs; or write us dire..t.

SHWAYDER BROS., INC., PUBLIC SEATING DIVISION
DETROIT 29, MICH.

YOU'LL SAY it really has a "Super-Top", when you see the remarkable resistance to damage offered by this new, low-cost Samson Folding Table! Tests like those shown *prove* this amazing table withstands the hardest use—more abuse than any other folding table you've ever known!

Use it indoors or outdoors—the beautifully grained top can take treatment that would ruin any ordinary folding table! Resists damage from spilled drinks, ink stains and hot dishes—wipes clean with a damp cloth!

Tubular-steel legs and frame make the Samson Super-Top strong enough to stand on. They're finished in lustrous, baked-on, chip-resistant enamel. See this sensational folding-table value at your Samson dealer's!

FOUR SAMSON COLORS TO CHOOSE FROM!

Green   Coral   Grey   Chartreuse

SHWAYDER BROS., INC., FURNITURE DIVISION, DETROIT 29, MICH.
Also makers of smart Samsonite Luggage

Samson Super-Top Table advertisement, 1950s, $8.00.

Card Party

Before the popularity of television, playing cards and listening to your favorite radio show was a familiar form of leisure activity. Playing cards or meeting the gals for mah-jongg, a Chinese game using tiles with different suits, were common pastimes through the 1950s. You would gather together neighbors, family members, and friends and enjoy a game of bridge, pinochle, canasta, mah-jongg, or perhaps poker. The collapsible bridge table with folding chairs was always on hand to use for card games. When you needed the table for other events, you might cover your card table with a quilted pad or tablecloth. It appears that baby boomers are rediscovering mah-jongg and are scooping up these sets along with collectors. Sets with Bakelite racks and ivory tiles are very collectible.

Leisure activities of the 1950s are also capturing the interest of teens, and poker has already had a comeback. Contract bridge may be the next card game revived. While preparing this section, I read an article in USA Today that said billionaires Bill Gates and Warren Buffet are trying to bring back interest in bridge. They have offered a million dollars to seed programs to encourage contract bridge in junior high schools. The American Contract Bridge League has set up a website, www.bridgeiscool.com.

Collecting playing cards has huge interest, and there are many collectors' groups that trade cards and share information about their collections. Every possible graphic has been used on playing cards, including themes related to advertising, famous people, transportation, geographical and environmental images, historical events, military, sports, and the arts. Not only do collectors look for unique backs of cards but they are also after cards with unusual fronts in which the design involves the suits, and cards with kings, queens, and jacks that represent fictional or famous people.

Values for decks of playing cards, like those for other paper collectibles, vary according to age, condition, rarity, design, and graphics.

Many of these decks can be found for $6.00 to $12.00, and prices climb higher for unusual cards. To learn more about collecting playing cards, contact the resource organizations listed in the bibliography.

Goren Bridgepoint Playing Cards, $6.00.

Tablecloth, embroidered, playing card theme, hot pink, $18.00 – 20.00.

Bridge table cover, quilted, $12.00 – 15.00.

Cookie tin, The Card Party, $6.00 – 8.00.

Junior Homemakers

Playing House
Sewing, Knitting & Home Crafts
Toy Mixers
Toy Pastry & Bake Sets
Children's Tupperware Sets
Junior Cookbooks
Junior Cookware Sets
Toy Kitchen Utensils

This is one of my favorite sections. I adore toy housekeeping and junior homemaking collectibles. Just like their mommies did, little girls had kitchenwares, such as tea sets, utensils, cookware, and bakeware toys. For children, taking care of dolls, sweeping the floor, washing dishes, serving tea, and "playing house" was playtime. Although these childhood pastimes were enjoyable activities, they were also important skills for girls to master for their roles to come as homemakers and housewives. When women married they were well indoctrinated for their jobs as nurturers and caretakers of the home and family. Books for young teens discussed important chores to learn, and home economic classes in schools were early training grounds for learning how to fold linens, make a bed, grease a baking pan, or diaper a baby. Even home sewing crafts were to be found in toy form. Toy sewing machines, knitting sets, sewing cards, and pot holder looms were very popular for little girls to practice being "just like Mommy."

Illustration, *Good Housekeeping*, December 1948, $8.00.

Playing House

Debby Dolls and Dollies paper dolls, box with contents, Jaymar, used, $15.00 – 18.00.

Ironing board, 1950s, pink and black, $15.00 – 18.00. Toy electric iron, 1950s, turquoise, $18.00 – 25.00.

Dollhouse, tin, 1950s, missing plastic windows and door, $45.00 – 65.00.

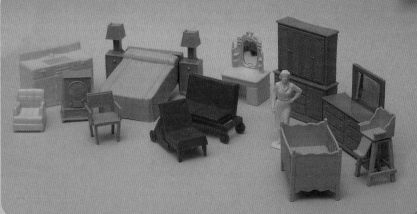

Plastic dollhouse furniture, 1950s, assorted pieces, $35.00 – 50.00 lot.

Sewing, Knitting & Home Crafts

Sewing, knitting, and home crafts often come in boxed sets that have covers that are more desirable than the contents. So it is not unusual to find collectors who are just after the graphics on the cover. Keep this in mind before you pass over an empty box or a sewing set that has been used or is missing parts.

Sewing with Laces, box only, no contents, $8.00 – 10.00.

Sewing cards, flowers, boxed set, partially used, complete, $12.00 – 15.00.

Knitting Nancy, boxed, complete, mint, made in England, $16.00 – 24.00.

Anne Orr Sampler Cards for Young Fingers, boxed set, unused, $12.00 – 15.00.

Picture Sewing book, early graphics, $15.00 – 18.00.

Pot holder loom, boxed, complete, $10.00 – 18.00.

My Knitting Basket, children's knitting set in plastic basket, $12.00 – 18.00.

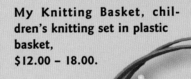

Playtime Tyndall Loom, children's weaving set, $15.00 – 18.00.

Toy Mixers

The toy cookware sets, utensils and accessories shown on pages 182 – 193 are from the collection of Jan Mansker of www.vintagetoykitchens.com. Jan has one of the most extensive collections in this area I have come across.

Mego Ware Super Mixette, 1950s, Japan, battery operated tin mixer, $25.00 – 35.00.

Sunbeam Toy Mixmaster, Jadeite bowls, 1930s, $1,200.00 – 1,600.00.

Baby Mixer, Japan, friction operated tin mixer, 1950s, $45.00 – 55.00.

Princess Mixer, Japan, battery operated tin mixer, light in the front, 1950s, $45.00 – 55.00.

Junior Homemakers

Micro-Mix, Micromatic Tool & Mfg. Co., battery operated mixer complete with original box, 1950s, $100.00 – 125.00.

Micro-Mix, Micromatic Tool & Mfg. Co., battery operated mixer and bake set, 1950s, $100.00 – 125.00.

Mix-ette Mixer, Japan, battery operated in mixer, 1950s, $60.00 – 75.00.

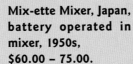

Junior Mixer, Alps, Japan, battery operated tin mixer with reamer, 1950s, $100.00 – 125.00.

Toy Pastry & Bake Sets

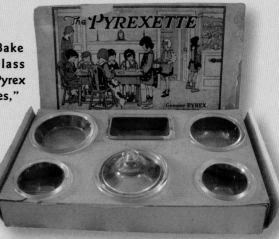

The Pyrexette Bake Set, Corning Glass Works, Genuine Pyrex "Like Mother Uses," 1920s, $250.00 – 350.00.

Sunny Suzy Glass Baking Set, Wolverine Co., blue tint Fire-King oven glass, 1950s, $150.00 – 200.00.

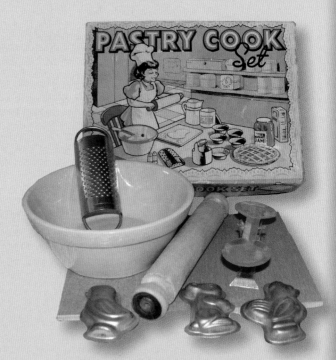

Pastry Set, Pressman Toy Corp., New York, includes Akro Agate bowl, 1930s, $225.00 – 275.00.

Pastry Cook Set, Berwick's, Liverpool, England, includes balance scales and yellow ware bowl, 1940s, $50.00 – 75.00.

Betty Crocker Junior Baking Kit, General Mills, includes baking utensils and mixes, 1950s, $100.00 – 125.00.

Children's Tupperware Sets

Tupperware Mini-Serve-It, Dart Industries, Children's Serving Set, harvest colors, 1979, $45.00 – 55.00.

Tupperware Mini Party Set, Children's Party Set, Dart Industries, 1987, $35.00 – 45.00.

Tupperware Mini-Mix-it, Dart Industries, Children's Mixing Set, 1979, $35.00 – 45.00.

Tupperware Mini-Party Set, Children's Party Set, Dart Industries, harvest colors, 1980, $45.00 – 55.00.

Junior Cookbooks

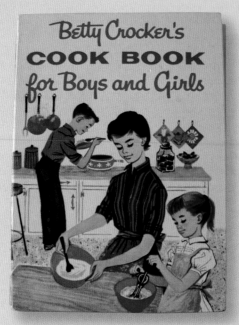

Betty Crocker's Cook Book for Boys and Girls, Golden Press, First Edition, 1957, $25.00 – 35.00.

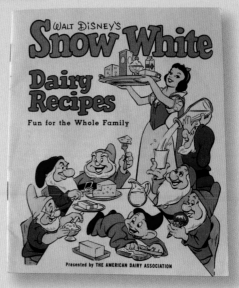

Walt Disney's Snow White Dairy Recipes, American Dairy Association, 1955, $15.00 – 20.00.

Cooking Is Fun, Miriam H. Brubaker, National Dairy Council, 1961, $15.00 – 20.00.

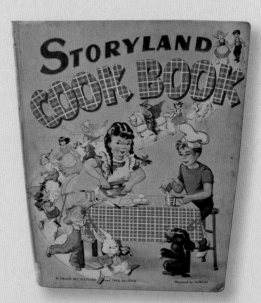

Storyland Cook Book, Helen Jill Fletcher and Jack Deckter, illustrated by Dorcas, Maxton Publishers, 1948, $25.00 – 30.00.

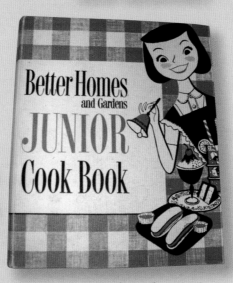

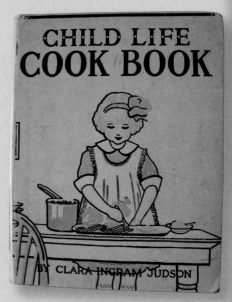

Kiddy Kook-Book, **Aluminum Specialty Co., includes aluminum cooking utensils and apron (see page 191), 1950s, $50.00 – 75.00.**

Better Homes and Gardens Junior Cook Book, **Meredith Publishing, First Edition, 1955, $25.00 – 35.00.**

Child Life Cook Book, **Clara Ingram Judson, Rand McNally & Co., 1929, $25.00 – 30.00.**

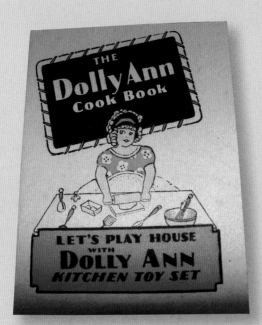

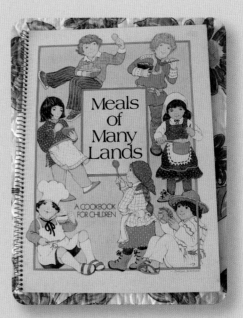

The Dolly Ann Cook Book, **included with the Androck Dolly Ann utensil sets, 1920s, $10.00 – 15.00.**

Meals of Many Lands, A Cookbook for Children, **recipes compiled by Miriam B. Loo, published by Current, Inc., 1978, $10.00 – 15.00.**

Junior Cookware Sets

"Like Mother's," Mirro Aluminum Co., cook and bake set with pressure cooker in original box, 1950s, $175.00 – 225.00. Below: Inside of box.

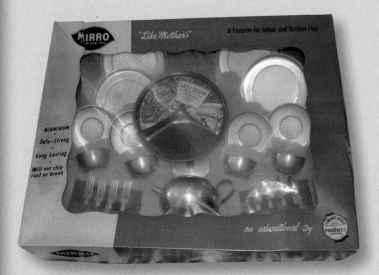

Left: "Like Mother's" tea set with lazy susan, in original box, Mirro Aluminum Co., 1950s, $150.00 – 175.00. Right: Inside of box.

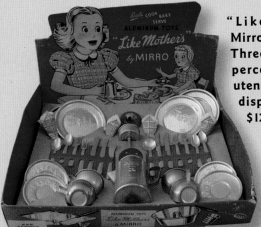

"Like Mother's," Mirro Aluminum Co., Three Little Kittens, percolator, napkins, utensils, complete in display box, 1950s, $125.00 – 150.00.

"Like Mother's" aluminum bake set, complete in original box, Mirro Aluminum Co., 1950s, $125.00 – 150.00.

"Like Mother's" bake set with covered oval roaster, Mirro Aluminum Co., complete in display box, 1950s, $100.00 – 125.00.

"Like Mother's" aluminum bake set with assorted cake molds, Mirro Aluminum Co., 1950s, $75.00 – 100.00.

"Like Mother's" Three Little Kittens aluminum tea set, Mirro Aluminum Co., original box with food cut-outs, 1950s, $75.00 – 100.00.

"Like Mother's" Three Little Kittens aluminum coffee set, Mirro Aluminum Co., original box with food cut-outs, 1950s, $75.00 – 100.00.

Alice in Wonderland bake set with tea kettle and original box, Aluminum Specialty Co., 1950s, $65.00 – 85.00.

Kiddy Kook-Book, Aluminum Specialty Co., includes plastic apron and cookbook box, (see page 187) 1950s, $50.00 – 75.00.

Copper Clad Stainless Steel Set, Revere Copper & Brass, Inc., includes Revere mini colander and bowl, 1950s, $175.00 – 200.00.

Small Fry Junior Cooking Set, Newburgh Metal Corp., includes Bakelite-like handled utensils, 1950s, $50.00 – 75.00.

Top: "Like Mother's" Picnic & Beach Set, Mirro Aluminum Co., complete in box, 1950s, $125.00 – 150.00.
Right: Picnic box with handle for Picnic & Beach Set.

Toy Kitchen Utensils

Kitchenette Quartette,
redwood handles, 1950s,
$20.00 – 30.00.

Little Homemaker Utensil Set, Wirecraft Corp., plastic
handles look like Bakelite, 1950s, $35.00 – 45.00.

Let's Play House Dolly Ann Kitchen Set, Androck, faces
painted on utensil handles, 1930s, $150.00 – 175.00.

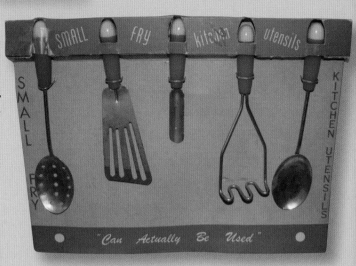

Small Fry Kitchen Utensils, plastic handles look like Bakelite, 1950s, $35.00 – 45.00.

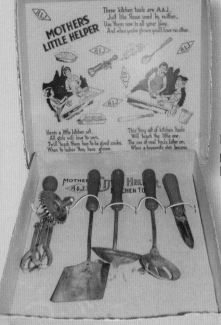

Mother's Little Helper Kitchen Tools, A&J, cute poems and graphics inside lid, 1940s, $150.00 – 175.00.

Soap Flakes & Detergents
Dyes & Removers
Laundry Products & Accessories
Ironing
Mothball Accessories
Beautifying the Bathroom
Broom Closet Essentials
Handiwork
Sewing
Fabric & Style Advertising

Of course the best things that happened to the drudgery of doing Monday's laundry was the arrival of the automatic washing machine in the late 1930s and the introduction of the top-loading washer in the late 1940s, as well as the automatic dryer at about the same time. Even with all the improvements in washing and laundry chores taking place in the colorful eras, some women still preferred to hang their clothes out on the line and spend their time ironing while they listened to or watched their favorite soap operas. These "soaps" as they are stilled referred to, were sponsored by major soap companies of the time, first on radio and then on television.

Laundry collectibles are always strong sellers. Many people like to decorate with vintage laundry accessories and buy these collectibles to create an older look. Other buyers of these items have become serious collectors of many different accessories and products available. Popular laundry collectibles are soaps, advertising boxes, laundry sprinkler bottles, irons, washboards, ethnic postcards, children's play accessories, embroidered laundry bags, and even clothespins of all kinds.

For an excellent resource on laundry sprinkler bottles, consult *Collectibles for the Kitchen, Bath & Beyond* by Ellen Bercovici, Bobbie Zucker Bryson, and Deborah Gillham.

"WON'T DADDY BE SURPRISED?"

The big new Norge probably *could* clean Daddy's hat, at that . . . for the big new Norge not only *washes*—it *rinses* and *dries for the line* as well! Oceans of sudsy water are set in motion by the action of the exclusive, feather-light Ro-ta-tor . . . garments are rolled down and around, time after time after time. And there are other advantages too: the roll-rim, non-splash tub; the steam-sealed, heat-hoarding cover; the non-clog drain; the final gentle "pressure cleansing"—advantages which result in far happier washdays and far brighter washes! Look in the classified section of your phone book for your nearest Norge dealer. He is waiting to tell you more about this washer, and about the other new Norge products too—all of them *products of experience*, precision-built and practical.

A BORG-WARNER INDUSTRY

Norge is the trade-mark of Norge Division, Borg-Warner Corporation, Detroit 26, Mich. In Canada: Addison Industries, Limited, Toronto, Ontario.

SEE NORGE BEFORE YOU BUY

Norge advertisement, *Ladies' Home Journal*, 1946, $8.00.

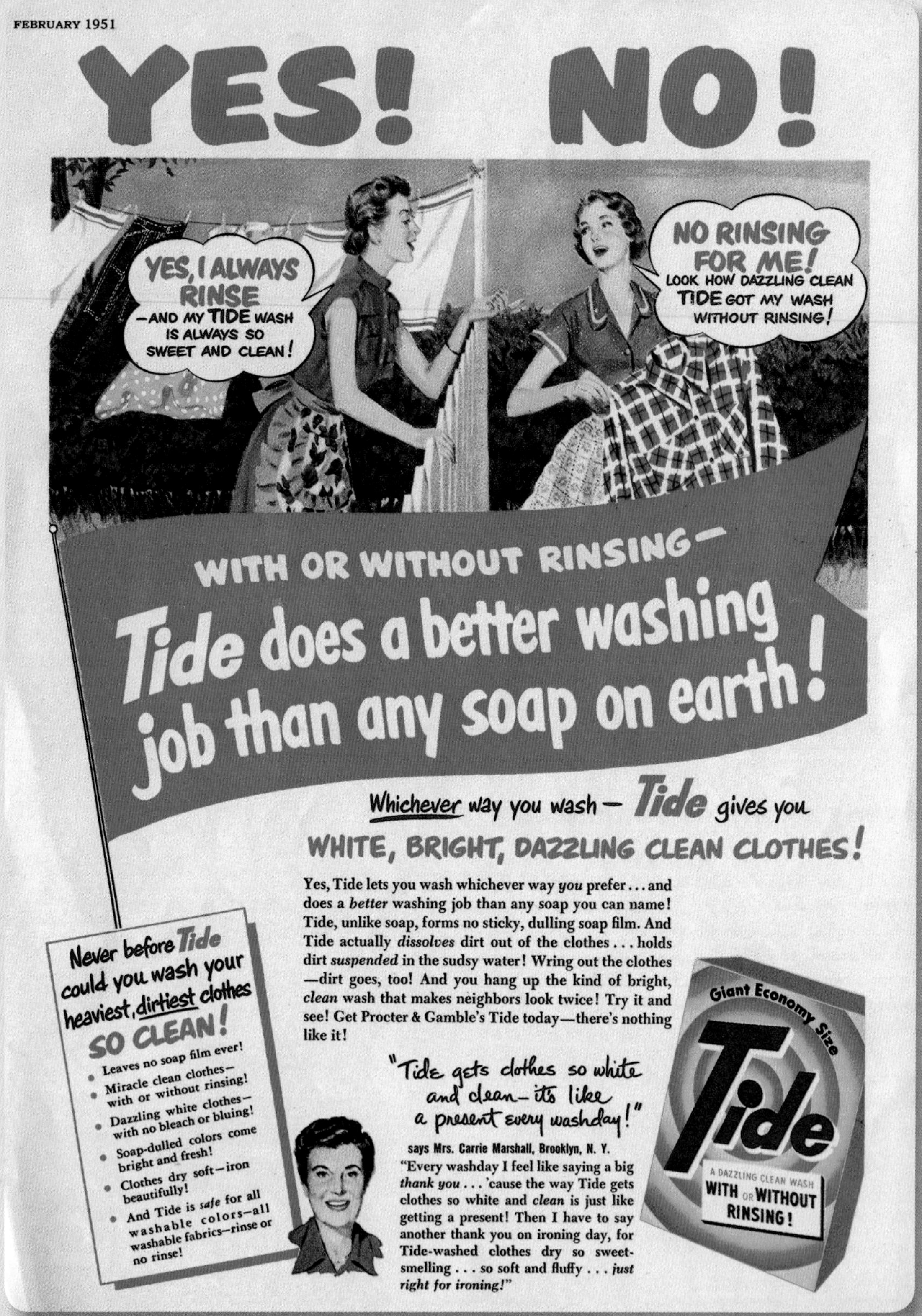

Tide advertisement, *Family Circle*, 1951, $8.00.

Soap Flakes & Detergents

The dime-store era saw tremendous changes in the way women approached laundry and washday chores. Earlier soap flakes performed poorly, leaving scum, dulling colors, and turning whites gray. Homemakers needed a lot of different agents to get clothes looking fresh and relied on bleaching, bluing, starching, and even dyeing fabrics when all else failed. In 1933, Procter & Gamble made big news when it discovered molecules called synthetic surfactants, which would change the nature of laundry products and thereby simplify washday tasks. These "miracle molecules" acted in two ways. One pulled the grease from clothes, while the other suspended dirt until it could be rinsed away. These newer discoveries were first introduced in a detergent called Dreft, which could only handle lightly soiled clothes. Later in 1933, Tide was created, and it could handle heavily soiled clothes. In 1946 Procter & Gamble launched Tide in test markets, to the housewife's delight. During its first 21 years, Tide was improved 22 times.

You will notice as you look at old soap flake advertisements and products that these cleansers were often promoted to be used for dainties such as nylons as well as for dishes.

Vintage laundry detergent boxes oftentimes are found at antique shows with a protective plastic shrink wrapping to keep them from going soft. This is because of the tendency of dampness to get into the laundry soap and seep into the cardboard box, creating quite a mess. It's no wonder that sellers take the time to protect these items, as the market for laundry products and accessories is hotter than ever. Prices will vary widely on these collectibles and seem to go up and down on eBay. True collectors of these items are looking for unusual and older products, handsome graphics, and other special characteristics, such as ethnic advertising. My experience has been that these unique soap boxes are apt to be found at specialty paper shows. For serious collectors or for those of you who might enjoy seeing an extensively photographed collection of soaps and detergents from the turn of the century through the later decades, along with values, consult *Washday Collectibles* by Pamela Apkarian-Russell.

Fab detergent, box with full contents, 7¼-ounce, Colgate-Palmolive Co., Jersey City, New Jersey, $15.00 – 25.00.

Rinso detergent box, 7¼-ounce, $15.00 – 25.00.

NEW IN DUZ! ONLY IN DUZ!

Amazing New EXTRA-DUTY FORMULA!

DUZ
SAFE SUDS! WHITER WASHES!

No other leading washday soap has it!

Never Before such White Washes with so much Color Safety!

There's a great new Duz in that famous big red box— and your dealer has it now! This amazing Duz with the new Extra-Duty Formula gives you the *whitest* Duz washes ever—and with greater *safety for colors* than *any* other leading washday package soap!

● No soap known gets clothes *cleaner* and at the same time *whiter* than new "Extra-Duty" Duz. Yet this same soap that gives such dazzling new whiteness to dingiest towels and sheets . . . the same soap that gets deep-down dirt out of grimiest overalls is actually *safest of all* the leading washday package soaps for doing pretty colored wash dresses, slips, everything!

● Get a box today—see with your own eyes how Duz does Everything on washday! Remember, of *all* the leading washday soaps, *only wonderful* Duz has this new Extra-Duty Formula.

Extra-Duty! Now Works Wonders Even in Hardest Water!

DUZ does EVERYTHING

IN THE FAMILY WASH!

Duz advertisement, *Woman's Day,* 1950, $8.00.

198

Bright Sail Soap Flakes, 12½-ounce, the Great Atlantic & Pacific Tea Company, New York, New York, $18.00 – 35.00.

Lux detergent box, 12½-ounce, with coupon for $2.00 off Fruit of the Loom half-slip, Lever Brothers, New York, New York, $25.00 – 30.00.

Ivory Snow box, 12½-ounce, Procter & Gamble, $15.00 – 25.00.

Sunny Suds box, "Softens Hard Water and Cleans Clean," Almo Soap Co., Camden, New Jersey, 10¢ size, $15.00 – 25.00.

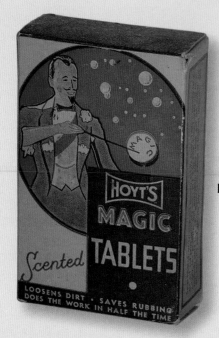

Hoyt's Magic Tablets, laundry whitening tablets, $12.00 – 20.00.

Whitex Wonder Bluing box, $12.00 – 15.00.

Yankee Perfume Starch, "Better, Quicker, Easier," 7-ounce, $8.00 – 12.00.

Staley's Laundry Starch Cubes box, $8.00 – 12.00.

Dyes & Removers

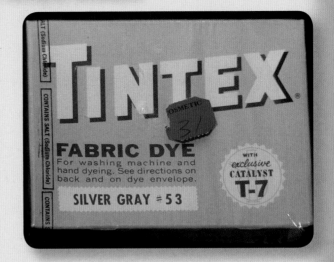

Tintex box, unused, $4.00 – 6.00.

Tintex box, unused, $4.00 – 6.00.

Perfection Dye package, unopened, $4.00 – 6.00.

Yankee Perfume Starch, Instant-Mix, 7-ounce, $8.00 – 12.00.

Laundry Products & Accessories

Wonderful for your baby's things.

It's easy to carry use and store.

Do your washing on the spot—*faster, cleaner* with Handyhot! Handyhot *Portable* Electric Washer is wonderful in apartments, or as the second washer in every home. It does "day to day" laundry with large washer performance!

Handyhot can wash up to 3 pounds of clothes in just 15 minutes. Washers from $26.95 to $39.95. Chicago Electric Manufacturing Company, Chicago 38, Illinois.

The Handyhot — Your Guarantee — *Gingham Package* of Quality

Handyhot *Quality Appliances*

Illustrated are 3 of over 25 Handyhot Appliances.
See them at better dealers Everywhere.

| **Automatic Iron** $8.95 | **Twin Waffle Iron** $12.95 | **Turnover Toaster** $4.50 |

Handyhot advertisement, 1948, $3.00 – 6.00.

Laundry sprinkler bottle, plastic, $8.00 – 12.00.

Sunbonnet Sue handkerchief holder. Soiled hankies could be kept in Sunbonnet Sue's pocket, ready for cleaning, $12.00 – 15.00.

Rinso advertisement, "New 1950 Rinso," $6.00.

Embroidered dish towel, laundry theme, $9.00 – 12.00.

Washboard, metal and wood, $10.00 – 12.00.

Felso advertisement, *McCall's*, 1952, $6.00.

Zippo Utility Line, encased plastic reel for drying hosiery, lingerie, and light laundry, $6.00 – 8.00.

Detergent holder, japanned, no markings, $15.00 – 18.00.

Coupons

According to the Coupon Council, an advocacy group of the Promotion Marketing Association (PMA), coupons began in late 1884 when Asa Candler, the druggist who bought the formula for Coca-Cola for $2,300.00, gave out coupons for his new soda-fountain drink. Coupons then became a favorite among cost-conscious housewives, who could find these handy promotions in the mail, attached to products, inside the boxes of household staples, or offered as part of other marketing programs. In the 1930s coupon use increased, as the Depression had drained American families and being thrifty was very important. The 1940s would see the proliferation of supermarkets, and coupons once used in the neighborhood grocery would continue in popularity in the larger grocery chains. In the 1950s, the Nielsen Coupon Clearing House was established and became the first company to be devoted to coupon redemption.

Laundry coupons, Duz and Dreft, $2.00 – 3.00 each.

Westinghouse advertisement, *McCall's*, 1949, $8.00.

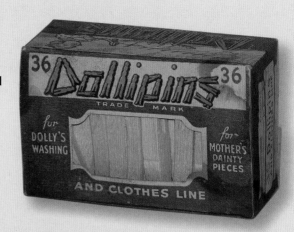

Dollipins, box with full contents, $6.00 – 8.00.

Push-On and Mastro Clothespins, originally sold for 25¢, Autoyre Comp., Oakville, Connecticut, plastic, 1949, $6.00 – 8.00 each.

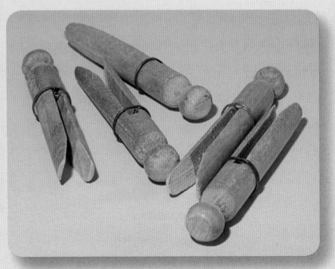

Clothespins, wood; lot of 20 – 30, $6.00 – 10.00.

Clothespin carrier, wooden clothespins are stored in a plastic-lined bag inside this cute children's plaid dress, $18.00 – 25.00.

Iron, Sunbeam, original box, English and Canadian advertising, 1940s, $22.00 – 25.00.

Travel iron, Universal, $12.00 – 15.00.

Glide-Tex press cloth package, "It Steams and Protects As You Press," originally sold for 59¢, $6.00 – 8.00.

Ironing

The electric ironer and product booklets from the 1950s shown here are from the Universal collection of the New Britain Industrial Museum (www.nbim.org). Booklets sell for $6.00 – 8.00.

If you want to buy an electric ironer, try looking online for companies that sell and repair vintage appliances. Other than at museums, whenever I have discovered these dinosaurs, the seller is usually too glad to have it carted away for a very reasonable price. If you would like to learn more about irons and ironing, try visiting www.jitterbuzz.com/contact.html

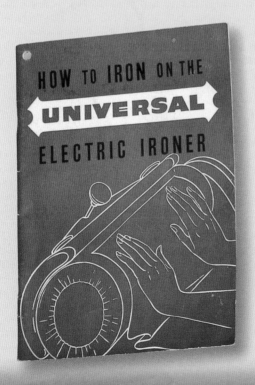

Mothball Accessories

Did you ever wonder why previous generations were so preoccupied with moth control?

From the 1930s through the 1950s, homemakers took many preemptive actions to prevent moth damage. Clothes were expensive in those days, and oftentimes handmade or bought to last several seasons. The last thing a woman needed was some pesky moth eating away at her clothes made of wool, silk, fur, feathers, or leather, favorites for moths. These animal-based materials were attractive garments for infestation, and homemakers knew that and were conscientious about using mothballs in their attics and closets. When textiles stimulated by war efforts (such as nylon, polyester, and others) were commonly available, the vigilance over moth control could relax. These fabrics are not breeding grounds for moths unless blended with wool. But until garments were manufactured in synthetic materials, mothballs or cedar closets were used.

Beginning in the early 1900s, cedar chests and, later, cedar closets were available and continued in popularity through the colorful eras. The Lane Furniture Company was well known for its cedar chests. One of my friends remembered how Lane would give out cedar vanity boxes to girls graduating from high school, to remind them to come back to Lane for hope chests and for other furnishings after they married. Today, climate-controlled homes, screens for windows, and advances in textiles have resulted in less damage from these little pests.

Expello moth tin, Judson Dunaway Corp., 1950s, $6.00 – 8.00.

Mothball tin, closet hanger type, $8.00 – 10.00.

These MOTHWORMS have got me licked! They chew up ALL our CLOTHES!

Dear madam: Don't give up! Help is at hand.

DON'T give up! Don't surrender to the mothworms! If all the old ways have failed, remember there is a *new way*, and its name is *Larvex*. It will change all your ideas concerning the prevention of moth damage.

If you have been trying to *hide* your clothes away from the mothworms in boxes or bags, you will be surprised to find that Larvex faces the danger *out in the open*, so you can let your clothes hang anywhere, ready to use without wrinkles.

On the other hand, if you have been trying to "smoke the moths out" with fumes or bad smells, you will be glad to find that *Larvex* is absolutely odorless, which is good news if you decide, in late Spring or early Summer, to wear again some garments you have already "put away."

The secret is that Larvex does not act on the mothworm directly. It protects the *wool itself!* It penetrates to the heart of the wool and then mothworms *can't* eat. So you see, you need not hunt the *mothworm* at all. No fear that you may miss a few! No fear of the moth eggs! One treatment by Larvex and the cloth is *mothproofed* against all these dangers.

Larvex is thorough and final. It will save you hundreds of dollars in moth damage and it is economical to buy. Think of it: Larvex lasts a whole year!

Ask for Larvex at drug and department stores. Odorless; non-injurious. It's a scientific triumph, in a class by itself. The Larvex Corporation, Chrysler Building, New York, N. Y. (In Canada: The Larvex Corporation, Ltd., Sainte Therese, P.Q.)

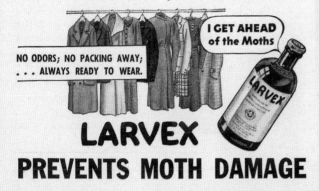

NO ODORS; NO PACKING AWAY; . . . ALWAYS READY TO WEAR.

I GET AHEAD of the Moths

LARVEX
PREVENTS MOTH DAMAGE

It's Here! A New LASTING way to mothproof!

ONE application of O-Cedar PERMA-MOTH protects for the life of the fabric

"IT'S WONDERFUL! . . . EXACTLY WHAT WE'VE BEEN HOPING FOR"

Here, indeed, is a new and sensational development! A new, *completely odorless, completely safe* way to mothproof woolens with *long-lasting* results. O-Cedar Perma-Moth, properly applied, remains effective *for the life of the fabric* . . . through everyday wear, brushing, repeated dry cleanings. In fact, you *re-apply* this amazing new mothproofer *only* if the fabrics are washed in water, or *wet* cleaned.

WHAT IT IS. O-Cedar Perma-Moth is a crystal-clear liquid, scientifically perfected and tested. Easily and quickly sponged on the fabric, it actually becomes *part* of the fabric . . . providing complete protection without the additional use of old-fashioned crystals, smelly preparations, special wrappings or storing. . . . Thus it saves you all the work of fighting moths with *temporary* methods—requires only *one* application.

Change to Perma-Moth *now*. . . . Use it to protect clothing, sweaters, blankets, upholstery, rugs. At leading stores everywhere.

NON-POISONOUS · Non-inflammable · Odorless · Stainless · Does not contain kerosene · Not removed by dry cleaning · Safe for any color or fabric not harmed by water.

O-CEDAR · CHICAGO, ILLINOIS · TORONTO, CANADA

O-Cedar's UNCONDITIONAL MONEY-BACK GUARANTEE

O-Cedar "THE GREATEST NAME IN HOUSEKEEPING"

Larvex advertisement, $3.00 – 6.00.

O-Cedar advertisement, *Woman's Home Companion*, 1946, $6.00 – 8.00.

Beautifying the Bathroom

Women were not only concerned with improving their own personal beauty, but they began in the 1940s to become more conscious of beautifying their homes. Bathrooms and vanity areas, like the kitchens of the 1930s, 1940s, and 1950s, were receiving more attention and becoming integrated into the overall décors of homes. Home magazines featured articles on how to improve various living spaces with wallpaper, textiles, and accessories. Color was now being added to bathrooms that were once white and sterile looking, not unlike early kitchens. Many of the companies that made tin kitchen canisters and range sets were also producing colorful bathroom ensembles with decorative wastebaskets, tissue holders, and shelving. Decals used on kitchenwares were made with bathroom designs and could be purchased to enhance powder rooms as well. Following tin wares, plastics emerged as materials for bathroom accessories. "His and her" towel sets were very popular in the 1940s, as well as hand-embroidered fingertip and guest towels. Homemakers often embroidered their initials on pillowcases and sheets and jazzed up other linens with handiwork. Flowers, bonnet ladies, and Southern belles were popular designs on pillowcases, textiles, and wall décor.

Atomic-era Influences

Although the majority of collectors seem to be after the softer, charming, and perhaps romantic look of vintage bath, bedroom, and vanity accessories, there is a growing interest in mid-century funky and whimsical styles. I have noted an increasing trend in collectors who want 1950s poodles, pixies, tropical fish, flamingos, and other retro designs. In fact, you would be surprised how many bidders there are on eBay for bathroom wall hangings made of chalkware or for other popular accessories of the atomic era.

"Have you seen what we've done to our home?"

Cottage color bathrooms from 1950s advertisements, $6.00 – 8.00 each.

Johnny said ..."Look, Mommy, how fast my boat sails down the tub"

... and I said: "Yes, son... and now you watch how fast the dirt goes when Bon Ami gets to work"

It's quick work... and it's easy work to clean your bathtub with Bon Ami. No hard rubbing—for Bon Ami cleans and *polishes* at the same time. No grit left in the bottom of the tub—for Bon Ami rinses away easily, leaving no sediment behind to collect in and clog up drains. And *no scratches* to dull the shining surface and make cleaning difficult. No wonder thousands of women agree there's simply nothing like Bon Ami for bathtubs and kitchen sinks.

Copr. 1936, The Bon Ami Co.

Bon Ami
for bathtubs

"hasn't scratched yet!"

Bon Ami advertisement, *Ladies' Home Journal*, 1936, $8.00 – 12.00.

Scouring Powders

Powdered cleaners, or scouring powders, were favorites in households during the colorful eras. Technically they are called pumicites, and they were used as scrubbing agents for sinks, stoves, tubs, and floors, as well as for cookware, especially porcelain or enamelware products, which were popular in the dime-store era. Their cleaning and polishing action is provided by fine particles of minerals, such as calcite, feldspar, quartz, and silica. Soap or surfactants are also included, to remove oil and grease films from dishwashing. Some of these products have bleach added to remove food, mold, and mildew stains. Some powders may have also added rust remover as well.

One of the most recognized polishing soaps or cleansers was Bon Ami, manufactured by the J.T. Robertson Soap Company of Manchester, Connecticut, around 1886. One of the main ingredients, feldspar, was originally discarded until it was realized that this soft mineral, when combined with soap, cleaned surfaces without scratching.

Bon Ami's famous logo, "Hasn't Scratched Yet," has become an advertising textbook slogan. How did the chick's relationship to Bon Ami come about? According to the company's explanation, "A newly-hatched chick will not scratch the ground for food for two or three days after it comes out of the shell because it is still living off the nutrients of the yolk. As neither chicks nor Bon Ami scratch, the chick is an appropriate symbol with the trademarked 'Hasn't Scratched Yet.'"

Sales of Bon Ami declined in the 1960s, and the product almost disappeared from shelves, but it returned under new acquisition in 1971. To boost sales, in 1980 the company launched a major advertising campaign with the headline, "Never Underestimate the Cleaning Power of a 94-Year-Old Chick with a French Name."

Scouring powder containers, assorted, Bab-0, Old Dutch, Klean-Rite, and Bon Ami, all in nice condition, $10.00 – 12.00. Bon Ami tins from earlier years will be priced much higher.

Kirkman Cleanser container, 14-ounce, Kirkman & Sons, division of Colgate-Palmolive, Brooklyn, New York, $8.00 – 12.00.

Lighthouse Cleanser container, featured an added lemon fragrance, Armour and Company, $8.00 – 12.00.

Octagon Cleanser container, Colgate-Palmolive, Brooklyn, New York, had a premium coupon attached that customers "young and old" could use for household products, $8.00 – 12.00.

Accept This LIFETIME METAL CLEANSER HOLDER

FOR ONLY 15¢

and windmill pictures from 2 cans of

New, Improved OLD DUTCH CLEANSER

A touch of brilliant color for your kitchen — no more need to hide your cleanser.

Beautifies the smartest baths — keeps cleanser in easy reach.

TO GET HOLDER FOR 15¢, DO THIS:

Here's a chance to try the remarkable, new *Improved Old Dutch Cleanser* you hear so much about these days. And get a colorful, unbreakable shaker-top holder that slips over and completely encloses the *Old Dutch* can—at an introductory bargain price.

This offer is good for a limited time only—and is made solely to induce you to try the new cleanser creation that astonishes all who try it. For new *Improved Old Dutch* contains a scientific grease-dissolving element and does these surprising things:—

(1) It cleans 50% faster than the famous *Old Dutch Cleanser* that has been America's favorite for years: Thus it puts an end to needless drudgery and elbow-fag—cuts cleaning time in half.

(2) The remarkable scientific agent in *Improved Old Dutch* dissolves stubborn grease almost like magic—gives *double-action* cleaning! Just a few quick wipes and sinks, stoves, bathtubs come sparkling—immaculately *clean!*

(3) New *Improved Old Dutch* is safety itself for porcelain, metal and painted surfaces. It *doesn't*

Wet-proof—keeps cleanser always free-running. No more clogged cleanser cans, no more wasted cleanser.

scratch—because made with safe, flaky Seismotite! Is really kind to hands—doesn't make them red or rough.

(4) Economical, too—you'll find grease-dissolving *Old Dutch* costs no more to use, month by month, than many harsh, gritty cleansers—because the Seismotite in *Old Dutch* spreads farther—each can lasts longer.

Accept Offer Today

This special offer is strictly limited and good only while supplies last. So try the new, grease-dissolving Old Dutch today. And send 15¢ and 2 windmill pictures, or labels, to Old Dutch for each holder you want. See coupon at right.

Choice OF 3 COLORS

CHINESE RED • WALDORF IVORY • JADE GREEN
Lifetime 30-gauge metal—won't break, chip or peel—baked-on enamel finish.
ENCLOSES OLD DUTCH CAN COMPLETELY

OLD DUTCH CLEANSER
DEPT. M-3, CHICAGO, ILLINOIS

Please send me _____ holders in the following colors:
_____ Red _____ Ivory _____ Green. I am enclosing 15 cents in coin and windmill pictures or labels from 2 cans of Old Dutch for each holder ordered.

Name_____

Address_____

City_____ State_____

(Offer good in U. S. A. only—while supply lasts)

OFFER LIMITED—MAIL COUPON TODAY

Old Dutch advertisement, *McCall's*, 1941, $8.00.

Broom Closet Essentials

Tidy House Super Waxed Garbage Bags, seven bags sold for 13¢, advertisement on the package said, "Modern Housewives Are Tidy," Tidy House Paper Products, Brooklyn, New York, $6.00 – 8.00.

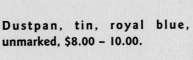

Whisk brooms, wood handles, $6.00 – 8.00 each.

Dustpan, tin, royal blue, unmarked, $8.00 – 10.00.

Handiwork

Women in the thirties, forties, and fifties commonly visited their neighborhood dime stores or variety stores to buy wool, fabrics, notions, and instruction booklets to make pot holders, sweaters, hats, afghans, quilts, pillows, curtains, and other handmade items for their homes and families. For needlework ideas, women could join mail-order clubs such as Aunt Ellen's Nationwide Needlework Club, which offered free transfer designs for pillowcases, tea towels, napkins, aprons, etc., to subscribers of its home-craft booklet, *The Workbasket*. Many notion companies also produced handiwork booklets offering homemakers instructions for many home and apparel projects.

Booklets shown in this section are all priced moderately and can easily be found from $3.00 to $8.00, depending on condition, graphics, and age. Recently there has been a return by women and even some men to home textile arts. Knitting and crocheting is back in vogue, and so is interest in these booklets. If you are buying these booklets for home use, it doesn't matter if the covers show signs of age such as slight tears and marks. However, if you are buying these collectibles for resale, be careful about booklets that have older price tags taped on them, because when you remove the tags, the tape often will damage the covers.

Embroidered Pillows

Vogart pillows and patterns are very desirable, and these thirties and forties collectibles create a big buzz on eBay when auctioned. The pillows had preprinted designs that were filled in with soft or pastel-colored dyes ready for homemakers to complete with hand stitches. Typically the pillows can be found with graphics of adorable puppies, cats, and children with big endearing eyes and busy at play. Vogart not only made pillow patterns, but it was also known for its popular embroidery patterns for kitchen towels, bibs, aprons, and other home textiles. The familiar days of the week dish towels featuring little kitty cats or puppies engaged in household tasks such as ironing, laundry, or washing dishes were popular Vogart products. Other Vogart patterns might include Mexican motifs, Dutch motifs, nursery rhymes, or kitchen themes such as teapots. Pillows should be free of stains and generally intact, although I don't mind a little edge mending in an otherwise fine pillow. Patterns are being reproduced and sold as "original" reprints of the old patterns; be careful unless you are looking for the pattern for home use and not as a collectible.

National Needlework Club advertisement, $4.00.

Edging & Tattering

All edging and tattering booklets shown here are valued at $3.00 – 8.00.

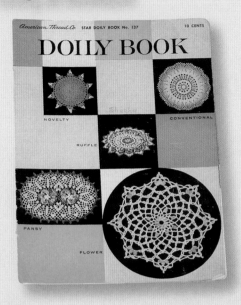

Knitting & Crocheting

All of the knitting and crocheting books shown here are valued at $3.00 – 8.00.

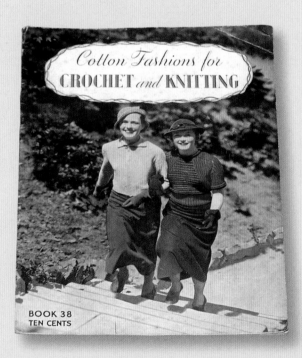

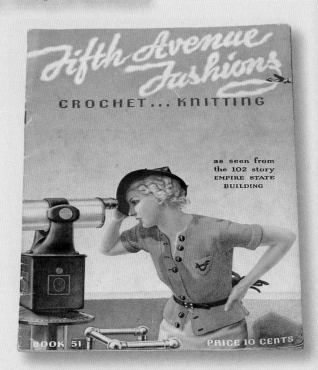

Embroidered pillow, Vogart, gray dog and yellow cat, $30.00 – 45.00.

Embroidered pillow, Vogart, two gray puppies over-looking brick patio, $30.00 – 45.00.

Embroidered pillow, Vogart, brown dog and gray cat, $30.00 – 45.00.

Pillowcase, Vogart, gray puppy sailing, $20.00 – 30.00.

Embroidered pillow, white puppy, looks like Vogart, $20.00 – 30.00.

Vogart Patterns

Assorted Vogart patterns,
$8.00 – 12.00 each.

Vogart pattern for aprons,
$8.00 – 12.00.

Vogart pattern, days of
the week dish towels,
$8.00 – 12.00.

Inside of the package
of the days of the week
Vogart pattern shown
above.

Sewing

During the war years women were encouraged to "take those old knockabouts and turn them into knockouts," keeping Uncle Sam happy and doing their part for victory. Sewing and mending were limited to using materials one already had in the home. Booklets were issued to help homemakers do this. In 1942, the Spool Cotton Company issued a red, white, and blue booklet entitled *Make and Mend: For Victory.* On the inside cover is the Consumer's Victory Pledge:

As a consumer, in the total defense of democracy, I will do my part to make my home, my community, my country ready, efficient, strong. I will buy carefully — and I will not buy anything above the ceiling price, no matter how much I may want it. I will take good care of the things I have — and I will not buy anything made from vital war materials which I can get along without. I will waste nothing — and I will take care to salvage everything needed to win the war.

(*Consumer Division, Office of Price Administration*).

During the war, women concentrated on restyling and revitalizing clothes they already owned by adding patches, crocheted trim, and collars, and by cutting up old coats and dresses to make new apparel.

Following the war, women did not need to be as thrifty with their sewing projects. Many notions were available at Woolworth's, which was indeed the sewing headquarters. The Woolco brand was a favorite, along with a vast array of notions, fabrics, and patterns. Today, sewing patterns from manufacturers such as McCall, Simplicity, Butterick, Vogue, and others are very easy to find, and they sell for $1.00 – 2.00 each. You can often buy these patterns in lots and pick them up at very reasonable prices. Besides using them for home sewing or collecting them for fun, some of my friends use them in their collage artwork or as scrapbook backgrounds. Patterns from the 1930s will cost a few dollars more.

In addition to fabric and patterns, many familiar sewing notions were bought at the five and dime, such as measuring tapes, pincushions, thimbles, zippers, fasteners, buttons, scissors, thread, needles, fasteners, elastic, and edging. Most of these notions can be found tucked away in old biscuit tins or sewing baskets at rummage and tag sales. Keep your eyes open for these goodies. Although you can usually pick up these items for a few dollars, collectors are now after the buttons and the more unique items, and sellers are becoming a bit savvy about their dime-store sewing treasures and prices are on the way up. To learn more about sewing collectibles, I suggest referring to references on the topic such as *Antique & Collectible Buttons* by Debra J. Wisniewski, and *Sewing Tools & Trinkets* by Helen Lester Thompson.

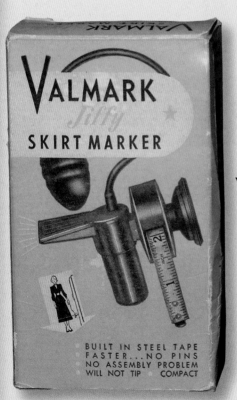

Valmark Jiffy Skirt Marker, $6.00 – 8.00.

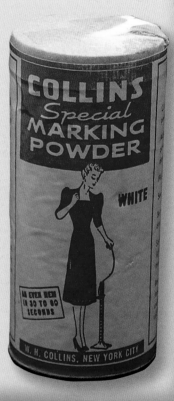

Collins Special Marking Powder, W.H. Collins Company, New York, New York, $4.00 – 6.00.

Circular knitting pins, original packages with contents, $3.00 – 8.00 each.

Sewing pattern, *McCall*, $2.00 – 4.00.

Make and Mend booklet, war-related sewing booklet to encourage women to help out with the war effort by mending clothes, patriotic red, white, and blue cover, $12.00 – 18.00.

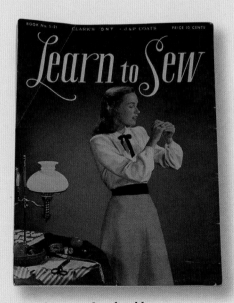

Learn to Sew booklet, $3.00 – 6.00.

Booklet, *The Home Handicraft Book*, $6.00 – 8.00.

Fabric & Style Advertising

Catalog promotional pages and fabric samples, Fashion Frocks, Inc., $10.00 each.

226

Stay-at-home FASHIONS

BE-DAZZLING PRINTS
GRACEFULLY
TAILORED FOR
GRACIOUS LIVING

STYLE 1517
Sizes 38 - 50
Price, $5.98

STYLE 1410
Sizes 10 - 20
Price, $5.98

Fashion Frocks

Please See Other Side

Beautiful at Breakfast
... AND ALL THROUGH THE DAY

STYLE 242
DRESS
Fabric: Jumbo Check (Cotton)
Colors: Clown Red;
Citrus Blue; Make-up Black
Sizes 12 - 40
Price, $3.98

STYLE 241
DRESS
Fabric: Gay Day Cotton
Colors: Honeysuckle Blue;
Dreamy Aqua; Minty Grey
Sizes 10 - 18
Price, $3.98

Fashion Frocks

Please See Other Side

MAKE **Contrast** YOUR THEME

FOR ALL SEASON
MAGIC

april 25th

Fabric: Miracle Butcher Linen
(80% Rayon—20% Cotton)

STYLE 132
Sizes 12 - 40
Price, $10.98

Fashion Frocks

Please See Other Side

227

Crib Toys & Accessories
Blankets
Nursery Planters, Banks & Figurines
Coloring Books
Wall Décor
Juvenile Textiles

intage nursery décor and products have become very popular and are climbing in value as collectors are actively buying these charming baby-boomer treasures. Now is the time to revisit your attic or your Mom and Dad's basement and unpack all those goodies that have been saved for generations.

Manufacturers have come up with lots of "vintage look" textiles, accessories, and décor. Juvenile lamp shades, diaper bags, crocheted items, dolls, toys, clocks, books, and wall décor have all been copied in recent years to resemble the originals.

Chenille pillows, blankets, and clothing are also extremely popular at this time. These items can be made from new materials that look old or from the original materials such as barkcloth or chenille made into new versions of the vintage look.

I would like to point out a few collectibles that are particularly of interest to collectors and are valued a bit higher than most of the more common products and accessories I have presented. Be on the lookout for ceramic baby dish warmers, old glass baby bottles, vintage textiles with juvenile patterns, and older children's books with full color plates.

If you love vintage nursery you will enjoy reading a fun book called *Flea Market Baby* by Barrie Leiner and Marie Moss.

Doctors and mothers agree... *Nothing better for Baby!*

Excerpt from advertisement for a baby formula popular in the 1950s, $4.00.

Crib Toys & Accessories

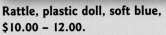

**Rattle, plastic doll, soft blue,
$10.00 – 12.00.**

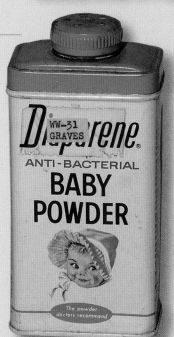

Powder tin, Diaparene, anti-bacterial, $8.00 – 10.00.

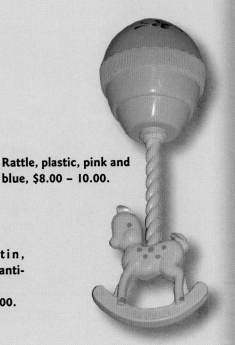

Rattle, plastic, pink and blue, $8.00 – 10.00.

BETTER BABIES

After Milk, What? Advice on food for your baby from the ages of one to five, weight and height tables, sleep, exercise, routine, clothing--in a leaflet, *Diet and Care of the Preschool Child*—5 cents.

Little Children's Meals to Plan? Here are menus for summer and winter, low cost ones too, recipes for simple sandwiches and desserts, all by an expert on child development. *What Should My Child Eat?*—price 15 cents.

Having a Baby? Our nine letters to a prospective mother help you with practical advice just at the time you need it. Give month when baby is expected. *The Expectant Mothers' Circle*—fee 50 cents.

First Year Is the Hardest—but we can help with monthly letters on care and feeding of the baby. *The Mothers' Club* —fee 50 cents.

Between One and Five: That's when questions of training and health come up and we have the answers in a set of leaflets—*The Nursery Club*—fee 15 cents.

Address Woman's Home Companion, Better Babies Bureau, 250 Park Avenue, New York City.

Women's Home Companion advice column, 1940s.

Vaseline, plastic nursery jar, full contents, 1950s – 1960s, $6.00 – 8.00.

Booklet, *Feeding Little Folks*,
toddler nutrition,
$4.00 – 6.00.

Changing table nursery set, plastic,
pastel yellow and aqua, held nip-
ples, cotton, swabs, and boric,
excellent condition, 1950s,
$20.00 – 30.00.

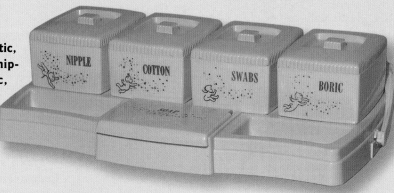

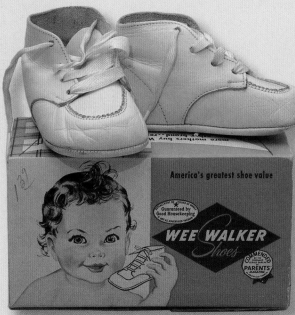

Baby shoes, Wee Walker,
box with contents,
unused, $15.00 – 20.00.

Clown doll, stuffed, blue gingham and red fabric, plastic face, excellent condition, $15.00 – 18.00.

Clown doll, stuffed, pastel colors, plastic face, excellent condition, $12.00 – 15.00.

Crib toy, stuffed rooster, made of soft plastic, perhaps oilcloth, primary colors, $12.00 – 15.00.

Squeeze crib toy, monkey, plastic, noisemaker, $8.00 – 12.00.

Cloth doll, $15.00 – 18.00.

Cloth doll, plastic face, plaid outfit, $30.00 – 45.00.

Cloth doll, $15.00 – 20.00.
Courtesy of Farm Village Antiques, Simsbury, Connecticut.

Cloth doll, $15.00 – 18.00.

Blankets

Baby blanket, Cotton Glo Plaid, lightweight, pink and blue, original label, $12.00 – 15.00.

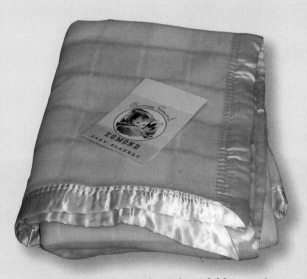

Baby blanket, Esmond, pink and blue, satin trim, unused, excellent condition, $20.00 – 25.00.

I Like My Supper

Is your baby one of those little darlings who relishes every mouthful or is he or she choosy about food?

It is really important for a baby to learn to like everything in order to get the good of the balanced diet that modern mothers plan. Among the cereals, breads, vegetables, fruits, meats, eggs, butter, milk, codliver oil that make up baby's meals are distributed the vitamins, minerals and body-building elements needed for growing, playing and feeling well.

To put your baby on the right track early remember these rules:

Cook children's food simply

Serve it lukewarm—not hot

Never serve gummy or lumpy or stringy food

Serve small portions

Give only one new food a day

Offer new food repeatedly till a child is used to it

Have meals at regular hours

PHOTOGRAPH BY
RUTH ALEXANDER NICHOLS

Mealtime should be a happy occasion

Women's Home Companion advice column, 1940s, $4.00.

Nursery Planters, Banks & Figurines

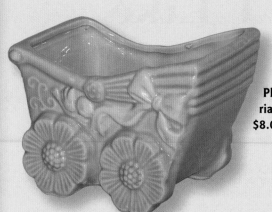

Planter, ceramic, carriage, blue,
$8.00 – 10.00.

Planters, ceramic, ducks,
yellow and pastels,
$18.00 – 20.00 set.

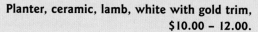

Planter, ceramic, lamb, pastels, $10.00 – 12.00.

Planter, ceramic, lamb, white with gold trim,
$10.00 – 12.00.

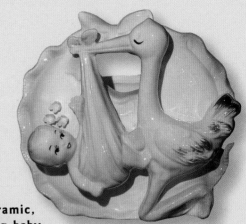

Bank, ceramic, yarn doll, unmarked, $12.00 – 15.00.

Planter, ceramic, stork holding baby, pink and blue, $10.00 – 12.00.

Bank, ceramic, cottage, pastel colors, $10.00 – 12.00.

Planter, ceramic, giraffe, pink and blue polka-dot, $10.00 – 12.00.

Planter, ceramic, dog, pink and blue plaid, $10.00 – 12.00.

1940s magazine illustration, $8.00.

Figurine, ceramic, boy with fish and cat, Grancrest Japan, $15.00 – 20.00.

Bookends, ceramic, children in garden, good condition, $25.00 pair; as shown (note chip on yellow watering can), $10.00.

Planter, boy with dog, $12.00 – 15.00.

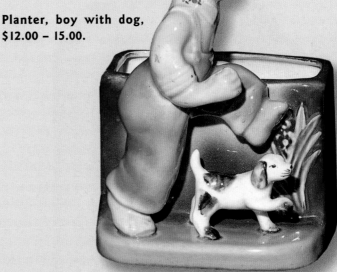

Planter, little cowboy, $12.00 – 15.00.

Coloring Books

Values of coloring books depend on condition, rarity, and graphics. These coloring books are mint and valued at $15.00 – 45.00. Photos in this section are courtesy of www.candyconnection22.ecrater.com

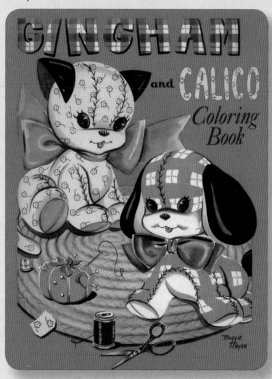

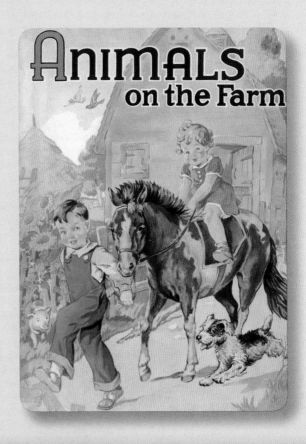

239

Wall Décor

Nursery Rhyme wall décor, two different sets shown, "Little Bo Peep" and "Jack Horner," $25.00 – 30.00 per set.

Juvenile Textiles

Barkcloth, cat and
yarn theme, one yard,
$10.00 – 15.00.

Fabric, heavy cotton,
ballet and bubbles
theme, "Inspired by
Little Lady Toiletries,"
54" x 47", 1950s,
unused, $10.00 – 15.00.

Cotton quilt cover,
reversible, polka dotted,
charming print, primary
colors, $40.00 – 50.00.

Dime-Store Beauty & Health

Dresser & Vanity Items
Hair & Nail Products
Medicine Cabinet Essentials
Powders & Fragrances
Half Dolls & Dresser Ornaments
Vanity Accessories

The 1930s through the 1950s were a very important time for the emergence of health and beauty products for women. Following the days of the flapper girl, women were coming of age and manufacturers who once focused on women with means were now extending their product lines to all. Dime stores were natural places for companies to promote their new affordable cosmetics, fragrances, and health items. Woolworth's led the way, carrying all the products that would now offer housewives an opportunity to look just like the women they admired on the big movie screen.

the Baldwins

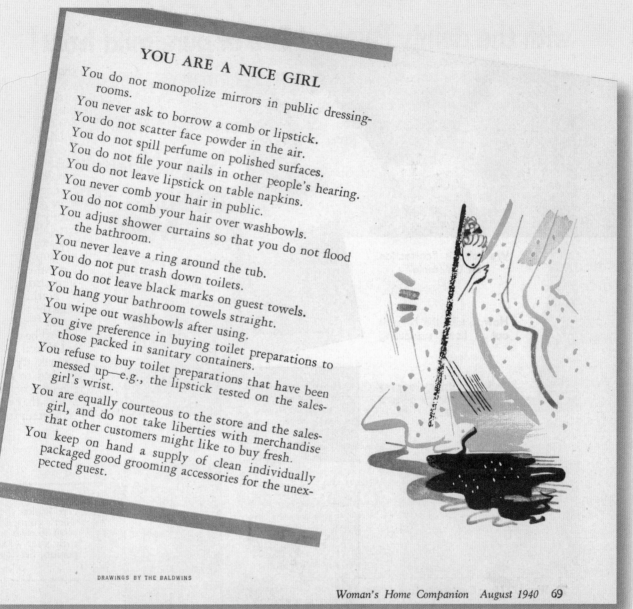

YOU ARE A NICE GIRL

You do not monopolize mirrors in public dressing-rooms.

You never ask to borrow a comb or lipstick.

You do not scatter face powder in the air.

You do not spill perfume on polished surfaces.

You do not file your nails in other people's hearing.

You do not leave lipstick on table napkins.

You never comb your hair in public.

You do not comb your hair over washbowls.

You adjust shower curtains so that you do not flood the bathroom.

You never leave a ring around the tub.

You do not put trash down toilets.

You do not leave black marks on guest towels.

You hang your bathroom towels straight.

You wipe out washbowls after using.

You give preference in buying toilet preparations to those packed in sanitary containers.

You refuse to buy toilet preparations that have been messed up—e.g., the lipstick tested on the sales-girl's wrist.

You are equally courteous to the store and the sales-girl, and do not take liberties with merchandise that other customers might like to buy fresh.

You keep on hand a supply of clean individually packaged good grooming accessories for the unex-pected guest.

DRAWINGS BY THE BALDWINS

Woman's Home Companion August 1940 69

Illustrations (on this page and the one preceding) from *Woman's Home Companion*, August 1940, $6.00 each.

LOOK! BEAUTY ON A BUDGET
with the dainty Personal Size of pure, mild Ivory!

Yes, wonderful
**PERSONAL SIZE
IVORY**
actually costs less than
other toilet soaps!

Beautiful to look at

Isn't it wonderful news that the same Ivory Soap you like best for your complexion now comes in a Personal Size to pretty up your bathroom? Its famous name says you've an eye for quality—your own lovely complexion proves you've an eye for beauty, too!

Beauty for you—That Ivory Look

Get some Personal Size Ivory today. It's the handy toilet soap size of gentle Ivory, the soap more doctors advise for baby's skin—and yours—than all other brands of soap put together. Change to regular care and use Ivory. In seven short days, your mirror will show you a softer, smoother, younger-looking complexion, *That Ivory Look!*

Beauty at a saving, too

Yes, you get 4 cakes of this wonderful Personal Size Ivory for about the same price you pay for 3 cakes of other well-known toilet soaps. Buy some today!

*More doctors advise Ivory
for skin care
than any other soap*

**4 cakes of
Personal Size Ivory
cost about the same as 3 cakes
of other well-known
toilet soaps!**

99 44/100 % PURE...IT FLOATS

Ivory advertisement, *Good Housekeeping,* **1951, $8.00.**

Dresser & Vanity Items

Cosmetic bags, purses, compacts, and vanity items would also blossom as essentials that women used to hold their lip balms, powders, lipsticks, colognes, perfumes, combs, and other popular sundries that they bought at Woolworth's. Besides special carrying cases for these articles, women could also find dresser accessories displayed near the cosmetic counters at the five and dimes. Trinket and keepsake boxes, dresser trays, powder jars, jewelry boxes, and make-up holders were popular purchases. These cherished dresser companions held jewelry, religious articles, make-up, combs, and brushes. Handkerchiefs, gloves, nylons, dainties, buckles, and hair ornaments might be kept in coordinating compartmentalized storage boxes.

These dresser ornaments and storage products were made from a variety of materials, including ceramic, wood, glass, silver, metals, Bakelite, celluloid, and later plastics. Visiting Woolworth's for health and beauty merchandise was routine for women during the colorful eras. Women visiting these stores often had their favorite salesgirls, who kept their eyes open for them for the latest lipstick or fragrance and were happy to introduce these products to their loyal customers. Women's magazines were packed with advertisements from manufacturers who wanted to capture the interest of readers and promote their new and improved lines.

Cosmetic holder, plastic, Cosmetic Wheel, originally sold for 39¢, $12.00 – 15.00.

Nylon box, quilted blue plastic exterior, $10.00 – 12.00.

Hair & Nail Products

Cotton Plucks, advertising tin, for manicures, "A Sentinel Product," Forest City Rubber Co., Cleveland, Ohio, $12.00 – 15.00.

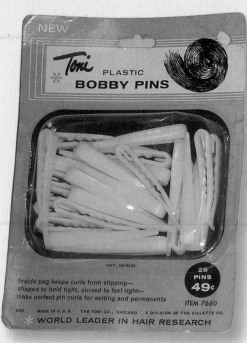

Toni Plastic Bobby Pins, package, full contents, the Toni Co., a division of the Gillette Co., $6.00.

Page Stropper, box with contents, Page Belting Co., Concord, New Hampshire, $8.00 – 10.00.

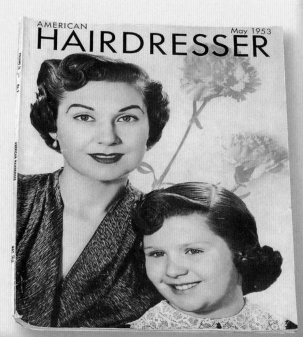

American Hairdresser magazine, 1953, $8.00 – 10.00.

Hair dryer, pink, hand-held electric,
box with full contents, Kenmore,
$18.00 – 25.00.

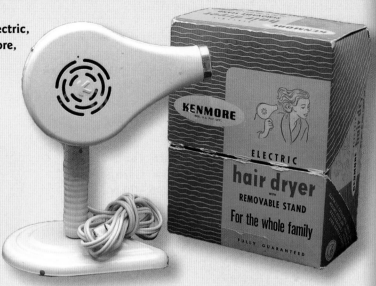

Fuller Brush magazine,
1950s, $6.00 – 8.00.

Hair dryer, Universal,
1950s – 1960s,
$15.00 – 25.00.

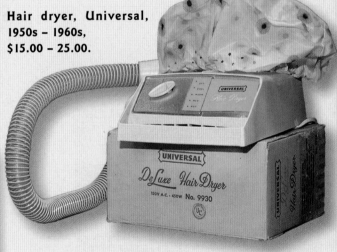

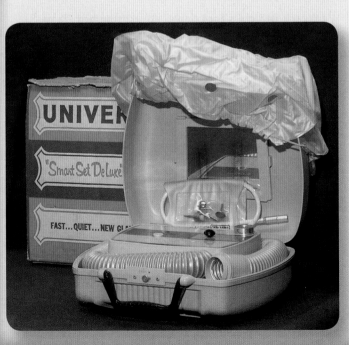

Hair dryer, Universal,
1950s – 1969,
$15.00 – 25.00.

Medicine Cabinet Essentials

Old drugstore and medicine cabinet essentials as well as vintage advertising in this area are hugely popular and of great interest to serious collectors and those who delight in creating the vintage look in their bathrooms. This is an area where there is a lot to learn, and you will often find a big range in what these items sell for. There are several older price guides available. Additionally you might enjoy reading Joey Green's *Incredible Country Store*, a delightful paperback about the "potions, notions, and elixirs of the past."

Resto Foot Cream, advertising box, $8.00 – 10.00.

Kotex, advertising box, International Cellucotton Products Co., Chicago, Illinois, $10.00 – 12.00.

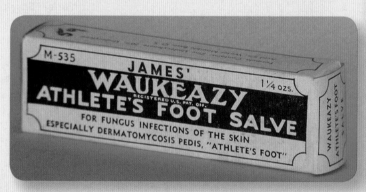

Waukeazy Athlete's Foot Salve, advertising box, James' Drug Co., New London, Connecticut, $6.00 – 8.00.

Vendol and SinaSiptec, advertising boxes with contents, $8.00 – 10.00 each.

Isodettes, advertising box, throat lozenges, original price $1.19, $6.00 – 8.00.

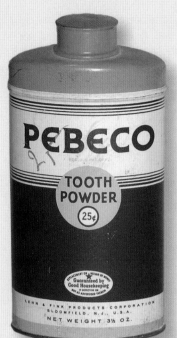

Luden's Menthol Cough Drops, advertising box with contents, $6.00 – 8.00.

Pebceo Tooth Powder, advertising tin, Lehn & Fine Products Corp., Bloomfield, New Jersey, $10.00 – 12.00.

Mennen Talc tin, $10.00 – 12.00.

Mennen Quinsana tin, $10.00 – 12.00.

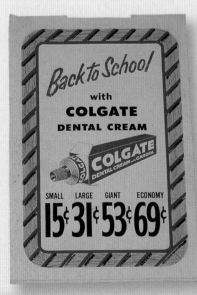

Old store advertising sign, Colgate toothpaste, $10.00 – 12.00.

Walpak toilet paper, package, $6.00 – 8.00.

Powders & Fragrances

Fragrance bottles with original labels and packaging are difficult to find and pricey at best. During holiday times especially, many families would visit the five and dime to find attractive boxed sets of their favorite colognes, perfumes, and powders. Evening in Paris, Coty, Ponds, Channel, Old Spice, Yardley, and many others were popular and frequently advertised in magazines. Coty's Emeraude fragrance was featured in a 1941 ad for $1.00 to $9.75 with accompanying dusting powder for under $2.00. In 1942, a boxed set of Evening in Paris would sell for between $1.00 and $10.00. Today a boxed set of Evening in Paris is not easy to find, and small individual bottles might sell for $10.00 – 25.00 each.

Spicy Apple Blossom Gift Set, $12.00 – 15.00.

Powder tin, $8.00 – 12.00.

Powder tin, $8.00 – 12.00.

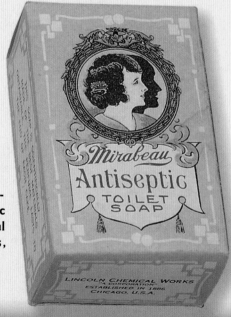

Advertising box, no contents, Mirabeau Antiseptic Toilet Soap, Lincoln Chemical Works, Chicago, Illinois, $4.00.

Lipstick holder, ceramic-skirted lady, $25.00 – 30.00.

Powder holder, ceramic, half-doll top, $25.00 – 30.00.

Planter/dresser ornament, ceramic, skirted lady with bonnet, $18.00 – 22.00.

Prayer lady, holder for rosary beads or keepsakes, $20.00 – 25.00.

Half Dolls & Dresser Ornaments

Half dolls, also called pincushion dolls, are cherished by many who collect these china, composition, or bisque ornaments that are commonly found with German or Japanese stamps or unmarked. They were most popular in the 1920s and 1930s, but were still produced and favored through the 1950s. Many of these half dolls have a flapper look or mimic the style of Marie Antoinette or Latin women. The German dolls are generally made with finer features and will be priced higher. Dolls with arms that extend completely from the body are also valued higher. Many of these dolls can be found with skirts or pincushion bottoms. To attach skirts, the doll's bottom half was pierced with tiny holes around its perimeter. Half dolls can be found with skirts, pincushions, plain, or sitting atop powder jars.

Prices vary according to age, condition, rarity, form, and dress. For more information, consult *Half Dolls Price Guide* by Sally Van Luven and Susan Graham.

Half doll with pincushion base, $25.00 – 35.00.

Half doll with pincushion base, $25.00 – 35.00.

Vanity Accessories

All of the collectibles presented here are originals, except for the handkerchief doll, which at first glance appears to have an old handkerchief for a dress. This indeed is one of those look-alike products that is charming in and of itself but is not the real thing. I have included it in this section to call your attention to the trend, which seems to be growing, of offering vintage styles in new materials.

Keepsake box, cedar, Valentine's motif, $22.00 – 25.00.

Handkerchief box, glass with ribbon trim, $24.00 – 26.00.

Towels, "His & Hers," boxed set, mint, $20.00 – 25.00.

Handkerchief doll, vintage look, not old, $8.00.

Sentimental Journey

Saving memorabilia in albums, once a hobby of older generations, has seen a huge comeback. Now even young mothers gather with other women enjoying the hobby of scrapbook making.

Today it seems that everyone is after ephemera, paper goods, holiday-related items, vintage graphics, decorations, and cards. Collectors as well as scrapbooking enthusiasts are all in search of yesterday's memories.

Once again this is an area in which reproductions are finding there way into the popular culture. Look-alike "vintage" valentines, cookie tins, and advertising are being produced and are easily confused with the real things by novice collectors.

I want to point out some of the hot collectibles you should look for. Cake toppers, vintage wrapping paper, old scrapbooks, wallpaper books from the fifties with atomic designs, Art Deco candy tins and boxes, and older cards with beautiful graphics are all desired and attract many bidders on eBay. Please note, however, that some of the paper-related items command higher prices on eBay than in local shops. (See the upcoming section on wallpaper books, page 285.)

Valentine's advertisement, *Family Circle*, 1950s, full ad, $8.00.

LADIES' HOME

JOURNAL

THE MAGAZINE WOMEN BELIEVE IN ★ FIFTEEN CENTS ★ DECEMBER, 1942

Christmas, 1942

Ladies' Home Journal **magazine cover, 1942.**

Christmastime

Christmastime during the 1930s, 1940s, and 1950s was a time of great changes that would have an impact on the way Christmas was celebrated for generations to come. Christmas decorations, ornaments, and greetings during the dime-store era changed from homemade and handcrafted to manufactured and mass produced. This was the beginning of the commercialization of Christmas. Santa Claus himself signed a deal with the Coca-Cola company in the 1930s to appear in print advertisements and promotions. Christmas trees, once chopped down from the backyard, were artificial now and ordered from mail-order catalogs or purchased in local five and dimes. Woolworth's made millions selling glass tree ornaments originally imported from Germany and then produced especially for Woolworth's by Corning Glass. More and more families moved further and further away from older customs such as threading cranberries or stringing popcorn to hanging tinsel and metallic trinkets on their silver aluminum postwar trees. Glass stars and premade angels sat atop silver or white trees placed on lino-leum floors next to Formica and chrome dinette and kitchen sets. Christmas was in the modern era, and even gingerbread cookies could be bought instead of made in the kitchen.

Christmas gift wrap, once an artistically inspired craft, would be forever changed and revolutionized by companies like Hallmark, which utilized cellophane wrap, offset printing, and gold stamping in 1936. In 1944 Hallmark's famous slogan, "When you care enough to send the very best," was launched and was yet another way that holidays were mass marketed instead of being celebrated as quiet homecrafted and family-based traditions. In 1953, Hallmark produced the first United States Presidential Christmas cards which began the trend of sending Christmas greetings around the world.

I suppose today many who rely on cyberspace to send out their greetings might actually long for the good ole days when sending and receiving festive holiday cards was in fashion. For now, one has to be thankful to receive all those animated charming and not-so-charming singing Santas and Chanukah dreidels that spice up emails at holiday time.

Good Housekeeping magazine photo, 1948, $8.00.

Vintage magazine, *Good Housekeeping*, cover with holiday theme, 1950s, $10.00.

Holiday window
stencils, premium with Ivalon
sponge purchase, 1950s – 1960s,
originally sold for 39¢, $6.00.

Ornament, plush toy, bendable,
Christmas elf, $6.00.

Ornament, plush
toy, bendable,
Christmas pixie,
$6.00.

Ornament, plush
toy, bendable,
Christmas mouse,
$6.00.

258

Christmas Cards

Postcard, Christmas theme, $3.00 – 4.00.

Christmas card, $3.00 – 4.00.

Christmas cards, assorted, 1940s – 1950s, $3.00 – 4.00 each.

259

Valentine's Day

During the dime-store era, children made their own valentines or assembled them from published kits, which might have included paper lace and cutouts. Die-cut mass-produced cards were also available, and children enjoyed exchanging cards in school.

Children's valentines from the 1940s and 1950s can easily be found on eBay and sell for $3.00 to $6.00 each or in mixed lots from $12.00 to $20.00.

In the thirties and early forties, candy boxes and tins had designs with Art Deco influences, often using colors of reds and blacks and gold or silver. Later tins would show more variety, and boxes would become more ornate, with lots of ribbons, trim, and ornaments. Heart-shaped boxes with elaborate covers of satin, lace, and flowers from companies such as Schraft's are very popular among collectors and can easily sell for $25.00 to $30.00 or more.

Candy & Cookies

Valentine's candy and cookie tins and boxes shown, $12.00 – 15.00 each.

Valentine's Cards

Valentine's cards, 1950s – 1960s, boxed, unused, $12.00 – 15.00.

Valentine's card, 1940s, $3.00 – 6.00.

HAT BY SALLY VICTOR

EASTER
SUNDAY
APRIL 21ST

The season's most popular messenger

Remember her on Easter with a Whitman's Sampler. She'll
be the proudest lady . . . proud of your thoughtfulness
in remembering her and remembering the day . . . proud,
too, of your excellent taste in choosing her dream candy,
the chocolates every woman knows are America's finest.

Whitman's
CHOCOLATES

CRISP ALMONDS covered in thick, dark
gleaming chocolate . . . a rich delight
to bite into. One of the many taste
thrills in your Sampler.

Copr. 1946, Stephen F. Whitman & Son, Inc., Phila

A WOMAN NEVER FORGETS THE MAN WHO REMEMBERS

Advertisement, Whitman's candy for Easter, $8.00.

Easter & Passover

Cookbook, *Tempting Kosher Dishes*, Passover theme, Manischewitz, $4.00 – 6.00.

Barton's candy box, $8.00 – 10.00.

Sweethome Chocolates, box
has blue, white, and gold
cover, Belle Rose Chocolate
Co., Boston, Massachusetts,
$15.00 – 18.00.

Alice Blue Chocolates, box has blue, white, and
gold cover, $15.00 – 18.00.

Biscuit tin, fruit motif,
Depression green back-
ground, probably 1930s,
$12.00 – 15.00.

Tin, Segal Fruits and Nuts,
$10.00 – 12.00.

Mother's Day

Candy & Biscuit Tins

Candy, cookie, and biscuit tins and boxes shown, $10.00 – 15.00 each.

Greer Garson notepad, $8.00.

Greeting card, $3.00 – 4.00.

Greeting card, $3.00 – 4.00.

Wrapping Paper

Old gift wrap used to be thrown out even before the tag sale. Sellers couldn't imagine that anyone would want paper that had been hanging around in Grandma's dresser drawers for decades. Now the climate for these paper collectibles has really shifted.

Vintage gift wrap is hotter than ever, attracting a great deal of activity on eBay and harder and harder to find in shops and at sales. I wonder if all the interest in scrapbooking is generating a renewed interest in wrapping paper. Keep your eyes open for these goodies; they are charming collectibles.

Packages or sheets of gift wrap shown, $8.00 – 10.00 each.

Bridal

Gift wrap and magazine shown, $10.00 each.

Wedding Gift Wrap

Packages or sheets of gift wrap shown, $8.00 – 10.00 each.

this exciting

Bouquet

1940s magazine photo, $8.00.

Cake Toppers & Ornaments

There has been an increasing interest in cake toppers in the last few years. Collectors are falling in love with these treasures, which have been around for quite some time. Sought-after types are the Kewpie couples or Kewpie dolls, which are celluloid individual dolls dressed in crepe-paper clothes. These were common in the early part of the century and sell for $50.00 to $100.00 when found intact and in good condition. Bisque cake toppers were made from the early 1900s through the 1930s and are generally marked "Japan" or "Germany." They are about 3" – 4" high and sell for about $10.00 to $15.00 for single pieces and more for sets. Very collectible are the War Brides. These World War II keepsakes were cake toppers with the grooms dressed in military uniforms. Military couples were made of porcelain, chalkware, or hard plastic and can sell for $45.00 to $50.00 or more. Grooms wore long black coats up until the fifties, when the style of dress changed and the coats became shorter. Cake toppers from the late 1950s through the 1970s are generally plastic and stand under silk flowers atop plastic bases. These modern brides and grooms can sell from $12.00 to $15.00.

Bridesmaid ornaments, plastic, pink and blue, $6.00 – 8.00 pair.

Bride and groom ornaments, $6.00 – 8.00 pair.

Cake topper, bride and groom, 1950s – 1960s, $15.00.

Magazine cover, *Ladies' Home Journal,* looking at the new baby, June 1946, $8.00 – 10.00.

A is for ANGEL
With short curlylocks.

B is for BILL
The Stork's and the Doc's

C is for CIGAR
Pop's passing 'em out

D is for DIAPER
(needs changing no doubt)

E is for EXEMPTION
On your Income Tax

F is for FORMULA
Make it up and relax

G is for GURGLE
Baby loves to do that

H is for HOSPITAL
where the "Arrival" was at

I is for INFANT
So tiny and small

J is for JOY
That is brought to you all

K is for KITCHY-COO
But that's baby talk

L is for LAUNDRY
Gotta do it – don't squawk!

M is for MOMMIE
Who tends every need

N is for NIGHT-TIME
And the 2 A.M. feed

O is for OUCH !
Be as careful as you can

P is for PATTY CAKE
BAKER'S MAN

Q is for QUIET
Baby must rest

R is for R-R-RING
Just hope for the best

S is for SAFETY-PIN
Now where did you park it

T is for THIS LITTLE PIG
went to market

Greeting card, new baby theme, $3.00 – 4.00.

Assortment of 1940s and 1950s children's birthday cards, $3.00 – 4.00 each.

Gift wrap, baby theme, 1940s – 1950s, $8.00 – 10.00 package.

Gift wrap, baby theme, 1950s – 1960s, $8.00 – 10.00 package.

Nursery scrapbook, blank, 1940s – 1950s, $12.00 – 15.00.

Birthdays

Nut cups, paper, ballerina theme, 1950s – 1960s, Hallmark, $8.00 – 10.00.

Children's record, party theme, the Record Guild of America, $8.00 – 12.00.

Mother Goose Drinking Straws, $6.00 – 8.00.

Candleholders, plastic, 1940s – 1950s, $8.00.

Outer Space paper cups, $8.00 – 12.00.

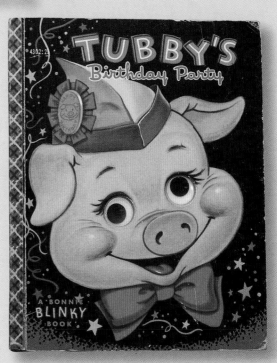

Children's book, *Tubby's Birthday Party*, 1954, "A Bonnie Blinky Book," worn condition, $6.00 – 8.00.

Donkey Party game, 1940s, Whitman, $7.00 – 10.00.

Dixie Cups, box with contents, $6.00 – 8.00.

Home & Kitchen Books, Booklets, Catalogs & Magazines

Home Magazines
Baking & Dessert Booklets
General Recipe Books & Booklets
Cooking with Electric Housewares
Appliance Booklets
Nutrition & Home Guides
Homemaking Books & Booklets
Kitchen Design Catalogs
Catalog & Stamp Plan Booklets

The paper collectibles shown in this section are in a very affordable price range. You can usually find recipe booklets and old homemaking guides and books in shops and at flea markets, tag sales, and secondhand shops. Be sure to look on Grandma's or Mom's shelves as well. Many families pass on their cookbooks and booklets, so you just may have a gem sitting in your own kitchen. In preparing this book, I bought some of the booklets on eBay and discovered after the fact that the prices online were much higher than the general market prices.

If you are searching for a particular paper collectible, you can also check out specialty paper or ephemera shows. I discuss these collectibles much more in the sections that follow.

Advertisement, *Good Housekeeping* magazine, December 1948, $8.00.

McCall's cover, February 1941, $10.00.

McCall's

OTIS L. WIESE, EDITOR

JULY 1940

NEWS AND FICTION
COVER PHOTOGRAPH BY HALLECK FINLEY

HOMEMAKING
COVER PHOTOGRAPH BY MADDICK-MEAD-HERRICK, FROM LOWNDS-EWING

McCall's table of contents, July 1940, $6.00.

By the twentieth century the food and kitchenware industry was booming, with many new and improved foods, methods of cooking, and kitchen appliances. Servants would soon disappear and homemakers would now be targeted by advertisers to buy all these new and modern products. At the same time, cooking schools and home arts were in fashion, and experts were often tapped to develop unique ways to utilize a new food product or appliance in meal preparation.

Cooking Experts

The foreword of the 1937 *Alice Bradley Menu-Cookbook* tells readers, "Alice Bradley is one of the best known food experts in the country, and Miss Farmer's School of Cookery in Boston, of which she is principal, has an unrivalled reputation." Alice Bradley took over for the famed Fanny Merritt Farmer upon Miss Farmer's death in 1915. Fanny Farmer, who started her own school in 1902 after working 11 years at the Boston Cooking School, her alma mater, is credited with turning around the way homemakers approached cooking and baking. Fanny taught her students to use precise measurements and accurate temperatures in the preparation of meals. This move to bring science into the kitchen was revolutionary at the time. It was no longer acceptable to use estimates in the kitchen such as "a little of this" or a "dash of that." Pinches, lumps, and handfuls were out and replaced with formulas that could be reproduced in the laboratory and published for others to follow.

In a 1932 booklet for Rumford Baking Powder, the introduction states, "These tests were carried on by Miss Bertha M. Becker, the well known food specialist, in her laboratory in New York. We wanted the opinion of an outsider, an unprejudiced expert, to either confirm or disprove results achieved in our experimental kitchen." Cookbooks and booklets during the colorful eras would all have similar introductions establishing the credentials and reputations of their experts and test kitchens.

Betty Crocker

While Fanny Farmer and her colleague Alice Bradley were real-life cooking experts, Betty Crocker is a persona developed by the advertising department of the Washburn-Crosby Company of Minneapolis, which made Gold Medal Flour, still the number-one flour even today. In 1928, the Washburn-Crosby Company merged with other major mills to become General Mills, consolidating the giants into the largest flour miller in the world.

Ms. Crocker was a fictional character created to answer cooking-related questions submitted by homemakers. Her last name was based on the name of a retired company worker, and her first name chosen because it sounded warm and friendly and would be appealing to housewives. Another company worker, the winner of a company contest, provided Betty's signature. In 1924 Betty Crocker got a voice when the first cooking show aired on radio. This was followed by a face in 1936, when artist Neysa McMein made a composite of the features of employees in the Home Service Department. Now the public was convinced that Betty Crocker, a fictional character, was a real person. She was so popular that housewives considered her the most important woman in American after Eleanor Roosevelt. This was precisely what the company wanted, to be able to link a credible expert to its products and test kitchens. Many recipe booklets and cookbooks bear the Betty Crocker name.

Another highly successful promotional strategy by General Mills is its Pillsbury Bake-Off contest, originally called the Grand National Recipe and Baking Contest. It was instituted in 1949 to celebrate the company's 80th birthday. Numerous cookbooks and booklets were published to share Bake-Off recipes and dessert features.

The Arrival of Booklets

Baking and entertaining were promoted in thousands of booklets and cookbooks, which flooded the homes of housewives during the 1930s, 1940s, and 1950s. All of these promotional and advertising products convinced the homemaker that cooking and baking were now easy and convenient. Mixing batters and kneading dough could be done with the help of an electric Mixmaster or, later, a hand mixer. Housewives were encouraged to make their families happy with delicious, laboratory-tested nutritious recipes created by experts in each company's consumer-oriented kitchen. Appliance companies often joined food companies in joint ventures to show how their newly improved kitchen appliances would make food preparation simple and dishes tasty and improved.

In the 1930s and 1940s, canned goods continued to dominate pantries, and more and more packaged products and convenience foods were available. In the postwar period, food enhancers and preservatives, as well as artificial tastes, were introduced. Prior to these advances, most food was bought in bulk, or at open markets or from peddlers and traveling salesmen. If a homemaker wanted to know if what she was buying was wholesome, she could look the food item over carefully or even hold it in her hand. Such was not the case with all these new packaged foods. In addition, the dime-store era housewife was being dazzled and sometimes confused with all the gadgets and electric appliances that were being introduced. Homemakers depended on the printed recipe and instruction booklets that manufacturers were only too happy to give away with their products.

Magazine Values

Besides individually written reference booklets to help housewives become familiar with new foods and methods of cooking, women's magazines were also a major way in which manufacturers advertised their new lines of foods and kitchen accessories. There were always regular columns on family nutrition, meal planning, and holiday cooking. Advertisements and graphics accompanying articles showed housewives clad in full aprons, wearing make-up, nylons, and heels — happily making soup, baking cookies, or warming up cereal for their children and thankful husbands. I encourage kitchen and home collectors to scoop up vintage women's or home magazines such as *McCall's, Better Homes & Gardens, Family Circle, Woman's World,* and *American Home* when you discover them. They are goldmines for teaching collectors more about the kitchenwares and collectibles they are buying. It is so exciting to see a full-page advertisement for Pyrex or Ransburg canisters, for example, and be able to view a product line and learn more about when these items were first introduced. These magazines are precious and can be easily purchased in small or large lots on eBay. Also, of course, keep your radar on when you are out shopping flea markets and shops. I recently spotted an entire box full of 1950s *House & Garden* magazines tucked under the table in an antique shop. The shop owner was only too happy to have me cart them away and sold them to me for a few dollars apiece. Home magazines can be found for $3.00 to $4.00 when part of a lot, or priced between $8.00 and $10.00 when sold individually. Magazines from the 1930s are more difficult to find than those of the later years and sell for more at times. Covers with famous people or special events, or illustrated by noted artists, are generally worth more, and consulting a reference book or paper dealer would be valuable.

Catalogs & Stamp Plan Booklets Values

Women spent a great deal of time in the kitchen during these years, but when they ventured out, it was sometimes to the five and dime store for housewares or to the Green Stamp Redemption Center to trade in their stamps for useful home gifts. Mail-order catalogs were also a favorite way to stock up on home needs. Sears and Montgomery Ward catalogs were sent out to homemakers seasonally and made shopping from home simple and convenient. Ordering from these huge catalogs, which stocked items in every possible category, was especially welcomed by families who lived a distance from department stores. Today online shopping has replaced the use of printed catalogs, which are becoming more and more a thing of the past.

Sears and Montgomery Ward catalogs can be found on eBay for $12.00 to $20.00. They are very plentiful some weeks and moderately available at other times, but they are out there and not that hard to find. Try to find ones with intact covers and good bindings. Beside S & H Green Stamps, there were many other stamp plans that gained popularity during the colorful eras. Stamp booklets, stamps, and premium catalogs are easily attainable on eBay and sell in lots or individually for $6.00 to $15.00.

Your

Subscription

EXPIRES

with

THIS ISSUE!

ORDER FORM

WOMAN'S HOME COMPANION
Springfield, Ohio

Please continue my subscription for the term indicated:

☐ **$2.00 for Three Years**

or

☐ **$1.00 for One Year**

I will pay on receipt of your bill ☐

Or, I enclose remittance in envelope with this card . . . . ☐

NAME_____

ADDRESS_____

CITY_____

STATE_____

Subscription price includes postage in U. S. and Possessions; also Argentina, Balearic Islands, Bolivia, Brazil, Canary Islands, Chile, Colombia, Costa Rica, Cuba, Dominican Republic, Ecuador, El Salvador, Guatemala, Haiti, Labrador, Mexico, Newfoundland, Nicaragua, Panama, Paraguay, Peru, Republic of Honduras, Spain, Spanish Possessions, Uruguay and Venezuela. For Canada, add 50 cents a year. For other countries, add $1.00 per year for extra postage.

Sept. 41 Final 740-H

Order form, *Woman's Home Companion,* September 1941, $3.00.

**FIRST
1-YEAR GIFT
SUBSCRIPTION
$3.50
Each Additional
*$2.00**

**SPECIAL
PRICE**

*Christmas
Gift*
ORDER FORM

*Your own may
be included

The American Magazine, Springfield, Ohio

I enclose $_____ for which enter subscriptions to The American Magazine for I year. Send notices on gift cards to the persons indicated below.

SEND TO_____   SEND TO_____

STREET_____   STREET_____

CITY_____ ZONE NO.____   CITY_____ ZONE NO.____

STATE_____   STATE_____

FROM_____   FROM_____

SEND TO_____   **SENT BY** _____

STREET_____   STREET_____

CITY_____ ZONE NO.____   CITY_____ ZONE NO.____

STATE_____   STATE_____

FROM_____

801

The **American** *Magazine*

Order form, *The American Magazine*, 1940s, $3.00.

Wholesale Product Catalogs & Product Booklets

Wholesale product catalogs, the industry's listings of its products, are different from individual product booklets for consumers that generally came accompanying a product such as an appliance. These smaller booklets are easily found and range in price from $8.00 to $10.00. Catalogs of product lines, used to promote particular manufacturers' lines to retailers or mail-order companies, are not that easy to find and are considered gems when they are discovered. These collectibles, which also include old Butler Brothers catalogs, are very desirable. They can be priced starting at $25.00 and go up in value depending on rarity and product interest.

Recipe Booklet Values

I have offered you a sampling of the types of booklets and books that were familiar to dime-store era homemakers.

I have grouped these booklets together according to the content of the booklets or books. I would like to point out a few tips for buying these paper collectibles. You will find that there are far many more 1940s and early 1950s booklets circulating out there than booklets from the 1920s and 1930s. Expect to pay more for the earlier booklets simply because they are harder to find and also more desirable because they are generally more attractive. Many times you will find that the earlier booklets have illustrations or artistic renderings of photographs, which are quite beautiful. Other early booklets may have been influenced by Art Deco designs, and these are much in demand. These booklets can be found for between $12.00 and $20.00. Certain subject booklets are also priced higher, such as early booklets on gelatin, baking powder, flour, chocolates, and spices. Cookbooks and booklets written by early culinary experts are valued higher than general ones. Most of the food-related booklets you will come across are really priced quite reasonably, with an average range of $6.00 to $12.00. The same price range holds true for appliance booklets.

Vintage Wallpaper Books — Hot, Hot, Hot

Before leaving this section I will also point out that wallpaper sample books, especially from the 1950s and with mid-century designs, are so sought after that you would be stunned to see them being gobbled up on eBay for hundreds of dollars. I am not kidding. I have participated in several online auctions and watched in amazement as 15 to 20 bidders actively tried to secure one of these retro sample books, which might end up selling for $150.00 to $250.00. My guess is that the winning bidders are in the design industry and are using these books to inspire future designs in home and fashion textiles and products. I am sorry to say I have no wallpaper books to show you in this section, but I sure would love to acquire some 1950s wallpaper sample books, and I will continue to keep my eyes open for these treasures.

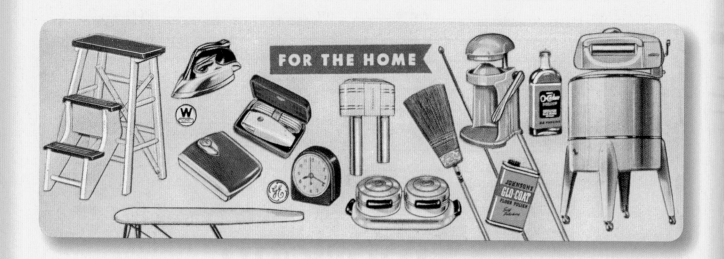

Home Magazines

(See pages 281 and 282 for values.)

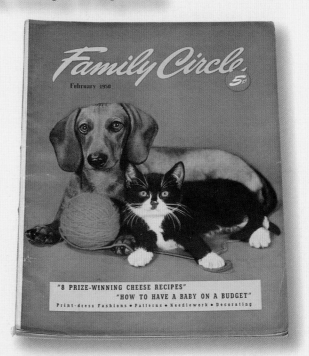

(See pages 281 and 282 for values.)

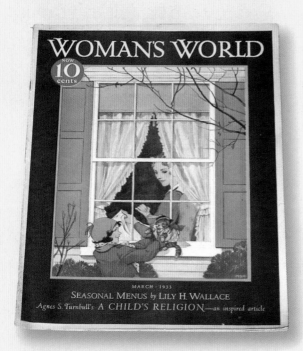

Baking & Dessert Booklets

(See page 284 for values.)

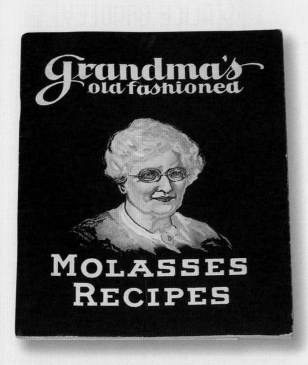

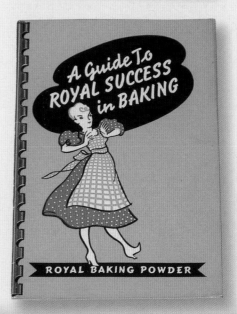

General Recipe Books & Booklets

(See page 284 for values.)

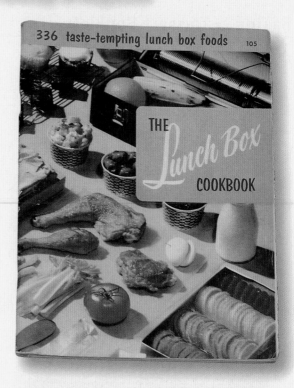

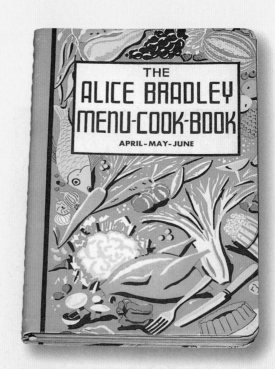

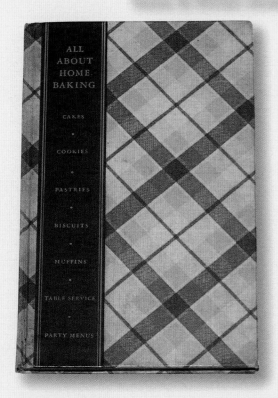

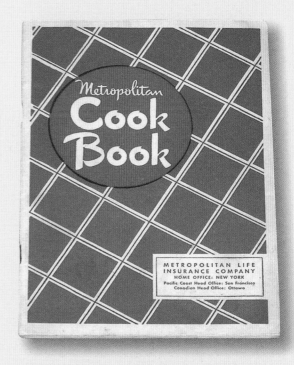

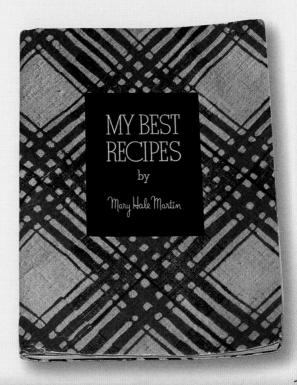

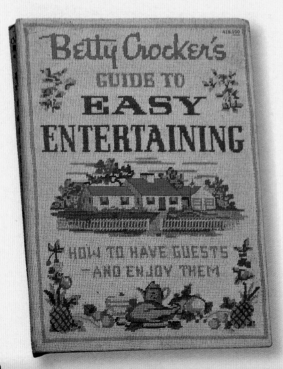

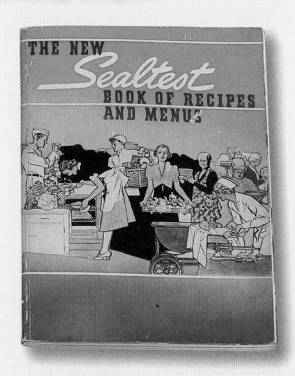

Cooking with Electric Housewares

(See page 284 for values.)

Appliance Booklets

(See page 284 for values.)

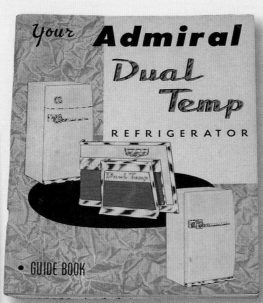

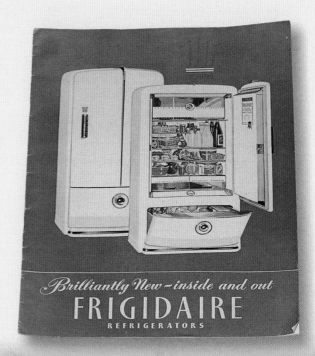

Nutrition & Home Guides

(See page 284 for values.)

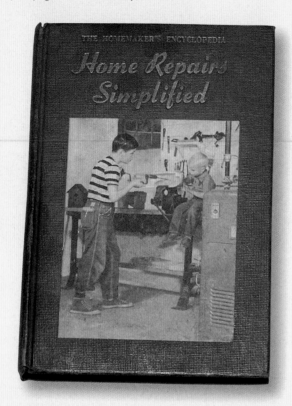

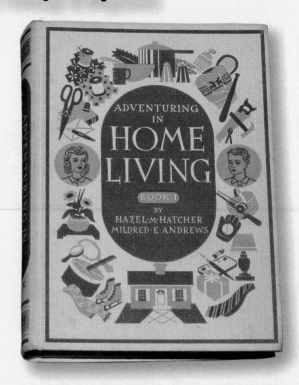

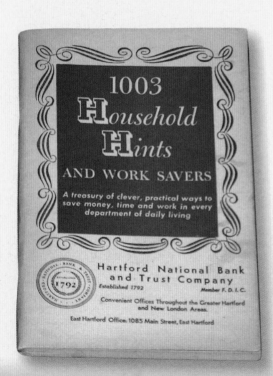

Homemaking Books & Booklets

(See page 284 for values.)

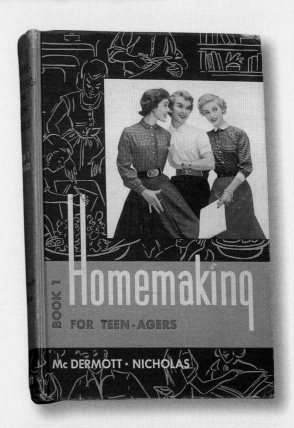

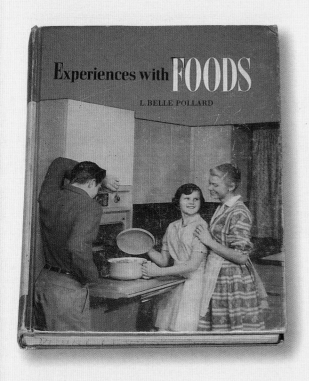

Kitchen Design Catalogs

(See page 284 for values.)

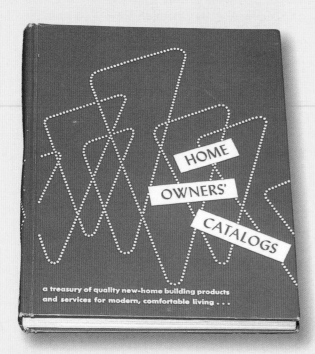

Catalog & Stamp Plan Booklets

(See page 282 for values.)

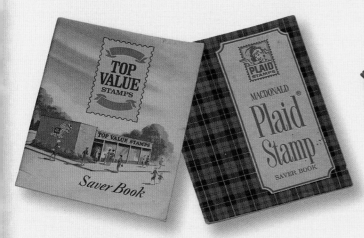

M'Call's

THREE MAGAZINES IN ONE

JULY 1944

OTIS L. WIESE
EDITOR

McCall's table of contents, July 1944, $6.00.

S.&H. Green Stamps advertisement, 1956, $8.00.

Why don't you get a discount for cash on your daily purchases?

...shop at stores that give you *S.&H.* GREEN STAMPS

WITH S&H Green Stamps you can get over 1500 nationally famous products for your home or your favorite hobby or sport. The latest models and designs of such famous companies as RCA . . . Ansco . . . Pepperell . . . Revere . . . Samsonite . . . to name just a few. And you don't pay a penny for any of these things!

Actually, S&H Green Stamps are given to you as a discount for paying cash. Many business men get discounts for paying

cash—so why shouldn't *you?* To get yours, all you need do is shop at stores that give S&H Green Stamps. Food stores, filling stations, department stores, drug stores . : . all kinds of stores . . . give S&H Green Stamps. And remember, it costs no more to shop at an S&H store.

S&H is America's oldest, largest, most reliable stamp plan —tried and proved for over 60 years. Be smart. Be thrifty. Start saving S&H Green Stamps today!

It takes only 1200 stamps to fill an *S.&H.* book. And these wonderful things you get by saving *S.&H.* Green Stamps don't cost you a penny.

ROGERS BROS. 1847

Kodak

Schick

MIRRO THE FINEST ALUMINUM

Spalding

PEPPERELL FABRICS

TOASTMASTER

The Parker Pen Company

EKCO

Bulova

Ansco

PYREX

UNIVERSAL

WE GIVE *S.&H.* GREEN STAMPS

START TODAY
Shop where you see this sign...

S.&H. GREEN STAMPS.
AMERICA'S ONLY NATIONWIDE STAMP PLAN

THE SPERRY AND HUTCHINSON COMPANY—SINCE 1896. NOW CELEBRATING ITS DIAMOND ANNIVERSARY

S.&H. Green Stamps advertisement, 1956, $8.00.

Bibliography

Allen, Colonel Bob. *A Guide to Collecting Cookbooks*. Paducah, KY: Collector Books, 1990.

Apkarian-Russell, Pamela. *Washday Collectibles*. Atglen, PA: Schiffer Publishing, 2000.

Bercovici, Ellen, Bobbie Zucker Bryson, and Deborah Gillham. *Collectibles for the Kitchen, Bath & Beyond*. Iola, WI: Krause Publications, Inc., 2001.

Bosker, Gideon, *Fabulous Fabrics of the 50s*. San Franciso, CA: Chronicle Books LLC, 1992.

Butler, Elaine. *Poodle Collectibles of the 50's & 60's*. Gas City, IN: L-W Book Sales Inc., 1995.

Celehar, Jane H. *Kitchens and Kitchenware*. Lombard, IL: Wallace-Homestead, 1985.

Colbert, Neva. *Collector's Guide to Harker Pottery USA*. Paducah, KY: Collector Books, 1993.

Crumpacker, Bunny. *Old-Time Brand-Name Cookbook*. New York, NY: Smithmark Publishers, 1998.

Cunningham, Jo. *Collector's Encyclopedia of American Dinnerware, 2nd ed*. Paducah, KY: Collector Books, 2005.

Daniels, Frank. *Collector's Guide to Cookbooks*. Paducah, KY: Collector Books, 2005.

Davis, Candace Sten, and Patricia J. Baugh. *A Treasury of Scottie Dog Collectibles: Identification and Values, Vol. II*. Paducah, KY: Collector Books, 2000.

____. *A Treasury of Scottie Dog Collectibles: Identification and Values, Vol. III*. Paducah, KY: Collector Books, 2001.

Erickson, Rick. *Royal Delft: A Guide to De Porceleyne Fels*. Atglen, PA: Schiffer Publishing, 2003.

Euans, Belinds. *PY/Miyao, Fun Kitchen Collectibles*. Grantsville, MD: Hobby House Press, 2003.

Florence, Judy. *Aprons of the Mid-20th Century: To Serve and Protect*. Atglen, PA: Schiffer Publishing, 2001.

____. *Gingham Aprons of the '40s & '50s*. Atglen, PA: Schiffer Publishing, 2003.

Franklin, Linda Campbell. *300 Years of Kitchen Collectibles. 5th Ed.*, Iola, WI: Krause Publications, Inc., 2003.

Glassner, Lester, and Brownie Harris. *Dime-Store Days*. New York, NY: Penguin Books, 1981.

Goldberg, Michael J. *Collectible Plastics Kitchenware and Dinnerware, 1935 – 1965*. Atglen, PA: Schiffer Publishing, 1997.

Heide, Robert, and John Gilman. *Dime-Store Dream Parade: Popular Culture 1925 – 1955*. New York, NY: E.P. Dutton, 1979.

____. *Popular Art Deco: Depression Era Style and Design*. New York, NY: Abbeville Press, 2004.

Huxford, Sharon and Bob. *Collector's Encyclopedia of Fiesta, 10th Ed.* Paducah, KY: Collector Books, 2005.

Ketchum, William C., Jr. *40's & 50's Collectibles for Fun and Profit*. Tucson, AZ: HP Books, 1984.

Lechler, Doris. *Children's Glass Dishes, China and Furniture, Vol. 2*. Paducah, KY: Collector Books, 1986.

Leiner, Barri, and Marie Moss. *Flea Market Baby: The ABC's of Decroating, Collecting & Gift Giving*. New York, NY: Stewart, Tabori & Chang, 2003.

____. *Flea Market Fidos: The Dish on Dog Junk and Canine Collectibles*. New York, NY: Stewart, Tabori & Chang, 2002.

Leybourne, Douglas M., Jr. *Red Book 9: The Collector's Guide to Old Fruit Jars*. 2001.

Lifshey, Earl. *The Housewares Story*. Chicago, IL: National Housewares Manufacturers Association, 1973.

Maloney, David J. *Maloney's Antiques & Collectibles Resource Directory*. Iola, WI: Krause Publications, Inc., 2003.

Matranga, Victoria. *America at Home, A Celebration of Twentieth-Century Housewares*. Rosemont, IL: National Housewares Manufacturers Association, 1997.

Mauzy, Barbara E. *Gay & Gifty Pot Holders*. Atglen, PA: Schiffer Publishing, 2002.

Bibliography

Miller, C. L. *Depression Era Dime Store: Kitchen, Home, and Garden.* Atglen, PA: Schiffer Publishing, 2001.

Milner, Melissa. "Fruit Jars...A History Worth Remembering." *Bottles and Extras,* Winter 2004.

Muncaster, Alice L., and Ellen Yanow. *The Cat Made Me Buy It!* New York, NY: Crown Publishers, 1984.

Outwater, Myra and Eric. *Florida Kitsch.* Atglen, PA: Schiffer Publishing, 2000.

Panati, Charles. *Panati's Extraordinary Origins of Everyday Things.* New York, NY: Harper & Row, 1989.

Plante, Ellen M. *The American Kitchen: 1700 to the Present.* New York, NY: Facts on File, Inc., 1995.

Plunkett-Powell, Karen. *Remembering Woolworth's.* New York, NY: St. Martin's Press, 1999.

Punchard, Lorraine May. *Child's Play.* Bloomington, MN: Self published, 1982.

Rosson, Joe. *Collecting American Dinnerware.* New York, NY: House of Collectibles, 2004.

Russell, Richard and Elaine. *Vintage Magazines Price Guide.* Iola, WI: Krause Publishications, 2005.

Smith, Timothy J. *Universal Dinnerware and Its Predecessors.* Atglen, PA: Schiffer Publishing, 1999.

Stille, Eva and Severin. *Doll Kitchens, 1800 – 1980.* Atglen, PA: Schiffer Publishing, 1997.

Thompson, Helen Lester. *Sewing Tools & Trinkets.* Paducah, KY: Collector Books, 1997.

Van Luven, Sally, and Susan Graham. *Half-Dolls Price Guide.* Grantsville, MD: Hobby House Press, 2004.

Wahlberg, Holly. *Everyday Elegance: 1950s Plastic Design.* Atglen, PA: Schiffer Publishing, 1999.

Ward, Peter. *Fantastic Plastic: The Kitsch Collector's Guide.* Edison, NJ: Chartwell Books, 1997.

Wisniewski, Debra J. *Antique & Collectible Buttons.* Paducah, KY: Collector Books, 1997.

Zimmer, Gregory R., and Alvin Daigle, Jr. *Melmac Dinnerware.* Gas City, IN: L-W Book Sales Inc., 1997.

Internet Resources

www.candyconnection22.ecrater.com

www.cottagerags.com

www.delfthuis.com

www.DoNotDestroy.etsy.com

www.elvisgrl63.etsy.com

www.etsy.com/shop/pinkgrapefruitstyle

www.fishlegs.etsy.com

www.ImSoVintage.etsy.com

www.jitterbuzz.com/contact.html

www.kitschykoo.com

www.LovethatVintage.com

www.madeonnantucket.com

www.modhaus.com

www.ModishVintage.etsy.com

www.monitortop.com

www.msdowantiques.com

www.nbim.org

www.onthecornervintage.com

www.padutch.com/hexsigns.shtml

www.preservecottage.com

www.randomretro.etsy.com

www.raraeaves.etsy.com

www.thebuttercup.etsy.com

www.TheWhiteMole.etsy.com

www.vintagegoodies.etsy.com

www.vintagetableclothsclub.com

www.vintagetoykitchens.com

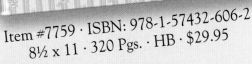